A PERFECT FIT

A PERFECT FIT

Luther Wright

GALLERY BOOKS | KAREN HUNTER PUBLISHING

New York   London   Toronto   Sydney

Gallery Books
A Division of Simon & Schuster, Inc.
1230 Avenue of the Americas
New York, NY 10020

Karen Hunter Publishing
A Division of Suitt-Hunter Enterprises, LLC
P.O. Box 632
South Orange, NJ 07079

First Karen Hunter Publishing/Gallery Books trade paperback edition November 2010

Gallery and colophon are registered trademarks of Simon & Schuster, Inc.

For information about special discounts for bulk purchases,
please contact Simon & Schuster Special Sales at 1-866-506-1949
or business@simonandschuster.com.

The Simon & Schuster Speakers Bureau can bring authors to your live event.
For more information or to book an event contact the Simon & Schuster
Speakers Bureau at 1-866-248-3049 or visit our website at
www.simonspeakers.com.

Designed by Renata Di Biase

Manufactured in the United States of America

10 9 8 7 6 5 4 3 2 1

Library of Congress Cataloging-in-Publication Data is available.

ISBN 978-1-4165-7097-4
ISBN 978-1-4391-9510-9 (ebook)

CONTENTS

Foreword by Karen Hunter   vii

Prologue   1

1   Opening Tap   9

2   Personal Foul   19

3   Hoop Dreams   29

4   Sandy   39

5   Please Don't Stop the Music   47

6   Elizabeth, I'm Coming to Join You!   53

7   Decision Time   65

8   Down the Hall   73

9   More Money, More Problems   87

10   Rookie Blues   97

CONTENTS

11 And All That Jazz   101

12 Out of Bounds   111

13 Blocked Shot   121

14 The Crack of Dawn   135

15 Falling through the Cracks   143

16 Fouled Out   151

17 You Are . . . *Not the Father!*   165

18 My God   173

19 No More Game   183

Afterword by Terry Cummings   193

FOREWORD

by Karen Hunter

I remember the first time I laid eyes on Luther Wright up close. I remember saying to myself, "That's the largest human being I have ever seen."

He was sixteen years old and already more than seven feet tall.

Luther was a junior at Elizabeth High School in New Jersey, and I was an up-and-coming sportswriter with the *New York Daily News*. High school sports was my beat at the time, and Luther Wright was one of the biggest names in basketball in the tristate area.

I covered his team for two straight seasons as they battled St. Anthony High School of Jersey City, which was one of the best high school teams in the entire nation.

I used to hate to have to interview Luther. As a reporter, one of the worst things in the world is to interview a one-word-answer subject. Luther was the king of the one-word answer—no matter what you asked him. Even when I would say, "Can you elaborate?" he would only say, "You know."

He finally warmed up to me a bit and would give me better quotes than he gave most. But it felt as though I were trying to break through this enormous wall. There were rumors that Luther was "slow." I often wondered if anyone was home.

But I later learned that Luther was very present. He was present, but he was mostly inside, hiding, looking for a place to be at peace.

On the outside, he sometimes seemed like a zombie. Even on the court, he appeared to be simply going through the motions. He had so much talent, so much potential. It wasn't just that he was seven feet two inches tall; he also had an athletic frame, nice moves around the basket, and a silky touch. He could dunk and shoot the ten-foot jump shot, but he did it all with little emotion.

That's why I was shocked the year he cried after his Elizabeth team won the Tournament of Champions— New Jersey's version of the Final Four, where the best teams from every division came together to settle who was indeed the best in the state. He cried like a baby.

I didn't know it at the time, but so much was behind those tears.

Like many who covered him, I had my opinions about him. I had him all pegged. Like many who covered him (and many who hung around him), I was wrong.

When he went to Seton Hall and I moved on to covering crime for the *News,* I would still keep an eye on him. I liked him. Something in his smile, which he didn't give too often, held more than I could imagine.

I once asked Luther, whom I would see with one of several girlfriends after a game over the couple of years I covered him, why he always went out with such short girls. His girlfriends would all hover around the five-foot mark.

"I don't want my kids to be big," he said.

That was a clue. This young man, for whom the entire world seemed to be waiting to shower with fame and fortune, didn't want that for a child of his own. This seven-foot-two-inch frame came with a burden that all of those who envied him could not see. When he told me that, I understood. For the first time I looked at him—beyond the height and the basketball glory—and I saw a young man who wasn't happy. I saw someone who seemed trapped in this huge body that everybody seemed to want a piece of—from college coaches and potential agents, from girls to guys who wanted to be popular just by being around him.

Still, it was in basketball, with its accolades, cheering fans, groupies, and "love," where Luther found stability and a home. But in 1996 it was all taken away. Actually, in a wave of self-destruction, Luther Wright threw it away. He was cut from the Utah Jazz, where he might have made a tremendous impact playing alongside Karl Malone and John Stockton. Luther went on a rampage that landed him in a mental hospital. His life spiraled into a wave of escapism. It started, even before his being drafted into the National Basketball Association, with marijuana and alcohol and women, then progressed under the pressures of being in the NBA to cocaine and then crack, leading to his release from the Utah Jazz in 1996.

I didn't hear about Luther Wright again until 2007, when an article appeared in the *Star-Ledger*.

The story began, *Luther Wright lay on an operating table and listened to the sounds of a surgeon cutting two frostbitten toes off his right foot.*

On the operating table that day, he lost two digits, but gained his soul. In that moment, as he heard pieces of his body being amputated, Luther Wright made a decision to change his life.

This is Luther's journey from growing up on the mean streets of Jersey City, never quite fitting in with peers, and sometimes even his family, to being a household name in his hometown with a multimillion-dollar NBA contract . . . to losing it all. His journey from a mansion in Utah to homelessness, feeding a crack addiction in Newark, New Jersey, is one for the ages.

But his overcoming it all is even more incredible.

Inspiring? Understatement.

PROLOGUE

ing. Ping.

It seemed to happen so quickly. I was on this gurney in an operating room of UMDNJ (University of Medicine and Dentistry Hospital in Newark, New Jersey). They had me numbed from the waist down and I was shot full of painkillers. But I was fully awake. I couldn't feel a thing as they cut off the toe next to my big toe on my right foot. I only felt a little pressure. And I didn't feel any pain when they cut off the toe next to that one, right down to the last knuckle. But the sound those toes made hitting the metal pan will haunt me forever.

Ping. Ping.

That was a part of me that I will never get back.

How had I let it get this bad?

More than two toes were being cut off that day. As I lay on that gurney, listening to them amputate my toes, high on whatever they gave me, I was more sober than I had been in years. This was the first time in a long time that I wanted to do something different with my life. For the past two years, I had been roaming the streets, homeless, getting high every single day or hustling to get money to get high. I didn't care about anything or anybody. I didn't want to hear from anybody. I just wanted to get high.

But as I lay on that gurney, listening to my body parts being cut off, I started to care about me. I was angry with myself for letting it get this bad.

When I thought about everything I had—money, a nice home, cars, women—and how I just let it all go . . . I didn't want those things back. I wanted me back.

With the eighteenth pick in the 1993 NBA draft, the Utah Jazz select Luther Wright. . . .

I was sitting in the Palace of Detroit, the home of the Pistons. I was sitting at a table with my mother, my stepfather, my agent (Sal DiFazio), and one of my boys from around my way. I was one of the few, the select few, invited to the draft. They only invited those expected to go at the top of the first round, and for those, like me, the NBA paid for them and their families to fly out. The NBA puts us up, fed us, and treated us like royalty.

It was a crazy draft. This was the year that most of Michigan's Fab 5, which made it to the NCAA Finals (when Chris Webber called that time-out), were coming out. Chris went No. 1 to the Orlando Magic, then was traded to the Golden State Warriors for Penny Hardaway, who went at No. 3. Shawn Bradley, who was bigger than I was at seven feet six inches (I never thought I would be looking up to anyone like that), went to Philly with the No. 2 pick. Also going in the first round were my boys Terry Dehere (No. 13 to the Clippers) and Bobby Hurley (No. 7 to Sacramento).

We made history that year. Terry, Bobby, and I were all from Jersey City. We all went to the same high school (St. Anthony) for one year. We all played on the same AAU team. And we were all drafted in the first round of the NBA in the same year. That had never happened before and has never happened since.

It was exciting sitting there. I didn't even mind that I was the last one of my crew to get picked. I was just happy to be there.

I was in the NBA.

When David Stern called my name, I jumped up. Kissed my mother, hugged my stepfather, gave a pound to Sal and my boy, and marched up to the stage to get my hat.

"Welcome to the NBA. Congratulations," Stern said.

But I'm sure he says that to every player drafted. I smiled for my photo with the commish and I met up with my family to celebrate.

That night Chris Webber threw a big party at the Fox. I took my man Christopher Garland, aka Sabree, and we drank and smoked and hung out with the girlies. I was on top of the world.

I had it all. I was excited about what was about to happen to me. At the same time, I was oblivious. I had no idea what was coming.

I went home and packed my stuff, and a day later I was on a plane to Utah with Sal to sign my contract and get ready for rookie camp. I had never been to Utah before. I couldn't even tell you where it was on the map. I had no idea and I didn't really care. All I knew was that I was going to play in the NBA.

When they called my name, I can't say that I wasn't disappointed. I thought I was going to be drafted by the New Jersey Nets. I just *knew* it. I had worked out for New Jersey. Willis Reed, the NBA great who was the general manager of the Nets, came in personally to watch me work out. I had a workout with Charles Shackleford and Jayson Williams—two of their star big men. I was all ready to suit up for the Nets and play for my home crowd, my fans, the same people who had supported me when I was playing for St. Anthony, Elizabeth High School, my AAU team, and Seton Hall University. Why wouldn't Jersey take me? It was a no-brainer.

But with the No. 16 pick, New Jersey took Rex Walters, a guard from Kansas. That summer, the Nets lost their star guard, Drazen Petrovic, in Germany in a car accident in which he was decapitated. So they needed a shooting guard and Rex Walters fit the bill.

I was told that Utah needed me. Their center Mark Eaton was gone, and I would be that final piece for Stockton and Malone to finally win a championship.

I had never really followed Utah or Stockton and Malone. I knew who they were, but I wasn't a fan and I couldn't tell you anything about them outside of their names. But here I was going to play with them.

As we were landing in Utah, I looked out of my window and could see snow-covered mountains. This was in the summer but they had snow. I thought that was cool. The whole city just looked clean and nice.

Then reality set in: "You have to *live* here!"

I had never lived anywhere but Jersey and was never more than ten minutes away from my mother's home.

In the hotel lobby, I noticed that I didn't see any black people, just whites and Mexicans. I started thinking, *What a country-ass town.* I saw people with cowboy hats and cowboy boots. *Where am I?* Utah. I found out it was run by the Mormons and they had their own set of rules. Rules I had no intention of following.

After I checked into the hotel, I decided to check out the local mall. Again, it was clean and peaceful. And again, very, very white. I don't think I saw a single black person—not on my way to the mall and not inside the mall. I didn't see my first black person until rookie camp. We had to do two-a-days—two full practices, one in the morning that focused on defense and one in the afternoon that focused on scrimmages—in rookie camp. That's where I met Bryon Russell. He made me feel welcomed and as if I had a friend there.

I was working hard—harder than I'd ever before worked. They were really pushing me. It wasn't the drills and the workouts. I was used to that. It was the intensity of the practices. It was the intensity of playing against guys who were either a little better than, a lot better than, or at least on the same level as I was. In high school, no one on my team could contend with me. In college, it was a little bit of a challenge but not much. I was still bigger and stronger than any other teammate in my position. But at this level, I was playing against Karl Malone and Felton Spencer every day.

I'd learned three things from my AAU coach, Sandy Pyonin, that helped me in the beginning: (1) Even though you worked hard today, you have to work even harder the next day because there is always someone else who is working on his game, and one day you will meet up with him. (2) You can't just turn it on or off. You have to practice as hard as you play. (3) You're either going to play hard or you're going to get your ass busted.

Those lessons came in handy whenever I got discouraged about how hard it was in practice. I was okay with it because I wanted to play. I was used to playing, and if this is what it took to play, then I would work.

I signed this contract for millions of dollars and I wanted to show that I could earn it, that I deserved it. They kept telling me that I was a project and that I wasn't really that good. I wanted to prove them wrong.

But I didn't.

1) OPENING TAP

I weighed eleven pounds and twelve ounces when I was born. At my birth was the first time of many that I made the newspaper. The *Jersey Journal* had an article about me being the biggest baby born in Jersey City that year.

My size was no surprise to anyone in my family. My moms is about five-eleven. My dad was about six feet three and a half. I have a cousin, Calvin Tillman, who played at Upsala College in East Orange, New Jersey, played pro ball overseas, and got a tryout with the Detroit Pistons. He was six-nine and skinny. My grandfather was seven feet two inches, like me. All of my uncles and cousins on my mother's side were tall. I have another cousin who is six-eleven. One of my female cousins, May, is six-three.

So the height wasn't a big deal in my home. I never heard, "Wow, you're so big!" among us. My family never harped on it. I never felt out of place in my home. But in public . . . once people found out how old I was, it was a big problem.

By the time I was three, I remember my mother getting into it with the bus driver because he didn't believe my age and wouldn't let me on the bus for the child's price.

By the time I started school, I knew I was different. I was always at the back of the line, of course. As I moved into the third and fourth grades, I could barely fit into the desks. I used to sit there and lift the desk off the floor with my knees. By the fifth grade, I was taller than my teachers.

The hardest parts of being so tall were the stares and people making me feel different. I was a kid, but I looked a lot older, and people would expect me to act much older. But I was just a kid.

Adults were the ones who usually made me feel out of place. My friends never did. When we played together, it didn't matter that I was a head or two taller than everyone else. You don't even think about those things until someone brings it to your attention. And you know there's always a wiseass in the bunch ready to pick on you.

Bigfoot. Lurch. Frankenstein. Goofy. Doofus. I heard

it all. And it all hurt. I would come home some days crying and my mother would say, "Don't worry about it, baby. Those are just words."

They didn't feel like just words. I was being teased for something I couldn't really help.

"Look at those feet!"

I wore a size eight men's shoe when I was eight. A nine when I turned nine. A ten when I was ten. When I turned fourteen, I graduated to a size sixteen shoe. Up until then, I was rocking the Hush Puppies, which went up to a size sixteen. But after I started wearing a seventeen in junior high school, my mother had to order shoes from Friedman's Shoes in Atlanta, Georgia. I still shop there to this day. Then basketball came along and I was able to get all the free sneakers I could wear.

But before then, it wasn't cool to be tall with big feet and big hands. Especially when I started going to public school. The kids were not only teasing me, but testing me. It was as if they wanted to see if I was as strong as I was big or as tough as I was big. I wasn't tough. But I wasn't a punk, and I wasn't going to let anyone push me around. So I was fighting a lot.

I never started trouble, and I had to be really pushed into it. But once I was pushed, I finished it.

They would start in on me on Monday, and by Wednesday we would be fighting. Ironically, they weren't cracking on me only because of my height. They also teased me because I didn't have the right clothes or sneakers. While I was in Catholic school, I didn't hear much about my clothes because that was easy. And my mother made sure that, although I was growing like a weed, I never wore high-waters and always looked presentable. But we didn't have money for the latest fads and styles, so I got teased for not being with it.

They also cracked on me because they knew my father collected bottles and turned them in for money. He had a job, but he also hustled to make ends meet.

In the summers, he had a truck and he sold watermelons. My father was known as the Watermelon Man in Jersey City. He made me work on that truck. That was a source of teasing. He figured I was big enough to be put to work and so he did. I worked on his hot dog truck, too.

I also got teased for going to church. My moms had me in church two to three times a week, including just about all day on Sunday. They called me corny and church boy. So I felt that I had to beat the hell out of them for bothering me. I didn't want to look like a punk.

It seemed as if I had a fight every day that first day of junior high. Looking back, I know I was ready and quick to fight not so much because of the teasing, but because I had a lot of anger and frustration building up inside that I needed to release.

A lot was going on in my life. My entire world got rocked when my parents split. I don't know what happened or what led to the actual breakup. I just know my mother came to me one day and told me to pack my stuff, that we were leaving. I knew not to ask questions. My brother and I packed up and off we went to the projects. It was the opposite of *The Jeffersons*.

I went from having this normal family, living in a decent neighborhood, going to Catholic school, to living in the projects with my mother, my brother, and on occasion an aunt and a cousin or two, and my grandmother Geraldine McDonald.

I used to visit my grandmother a lot in the Booker T. Washington projects. I loved visiting her house because you know how your grandmother can always make you feel special, and you can get away with things with your grandmother that you could never get away with at home. Well, it was a different story living with her. You know the saying about its being a nice place to visit, but you wouldn't want to live there . . .

Living with my grandmother, we had to live by her rules. It was harder on my mother than it was for me because my mother definitely didn't want to live there, but she had no place to go after she left my father.

My grandmother was no-nonsense. She smoked Pall Mall and chewed Cannon Ball tobacco. From Wadesboro, North Carolina, she was Cherokee, about five-ten, and had some meat on her bones. She was also a gunslinger, known to pack a .22-caliber gun.

I loved my grandmother because she was a real person. She loved her family. She loved the Lord. But if you crossed her or crossed her family, she would deal with you. I heard stories about how she used to handle people back in the day. A bullet hole in the wall of her apartment marked when she allegedly shot at her husband.

He didn't come home one night. The next night, he came to the dinner table expecting to eat as if nothing happened, and my grandmother came out and shot at him. The bullet grazed him. She kept that hole in the wall to remind him (and to remind the rest of us) of what she was capable of. If she raised her voice, you better duck. She had no problem getting the belt on any of us kids. If Mama McDonald told you to do something and you didn't do it, you better know what was coming.

My grandmother was unique. She was hard, but had a soft spot for her family and for people. If she could help you, she would. She wouldn't give you money, but she'd make you something to eat. She was known around the Booker T. Washington projects as that woman. If people had a problem, they would come to my grandmother and she would pray with them and feed them. She didn't have much, but she taught my mother how to stretch what they had—flour, sugar, cornmeal, grits, salt, pepper. You could grab something and make a meal. My grandmother was resourceful.

She had a real soft spot for me. I was her boo-boo, which meant she rescued me on many occasions. Under her roof, she was the law. She overruled my mother in a lot of things, even when my mother wanted to whup my ass.

"You ain't whupping that boy," she would say.

• • •

My grandmother had these rules, and they applied to everybody. We had to eat at a certain time. You couldn't watch TV when you wanted. And you couldn't watch what you wanted to watch.

I'd want to watch *Benny Hill*. But she wasn't having it. She would have us watching some western or *Dallas* or one of her soap operas or the *Six Million Dollar Man* and *Wonder Woman*. I'd be in the middle of watching Popeye or Woody Woodpecker and here she'd come.

"Boy, turn to channel seven, my soaps are on!"

I'd have to turn to *All My Children* or *One Life to Live* or *General Hospital*. I got real acquainted with the Luke and Laura saga.

One show I did appreciate my grandmother making us watch—*Roots*. At first, I was like "Oh, come on!" (to myself, of course). But as I watched the miniseries, it changed the way I looked at a lot of things. *Roots* definitely added something to my life.

I enjoyed watching that.

Living with my grandmother was also hard for me because I no longer had my own space. I had to sleep on the couch in the living room. My grandmother didn't have much room—only two bedrooms. Six, sometimes seven, of us shared those two bedrooms and one bathroom.

I missed my father, too. I missed hearing him say, "Junior, come here!" I missed his voice, his presence.

That was my daddy. And no matter what, I loved him. During the first few years after he and my mom split up, I definitely missed him.

Outside of the ass whippings, he was a good guy. My father and I had a crazy relationship. I'm glad I got to know him when I got older and understand him and appreciate the things he did for us. I loved my pops. I missed him then and I miss him now.

I love music because of my father. He exposed me to it at an early age. He also taught me about being a man—things I couldn't grasp then, but that I reflect on and understand now, such as how and why he got up every day and worked so hard for us.

Living with my grandmother was a big adjustment. But I was used to making adjustments to fit in.

Public school was a huge change. Everything was different. We didn't have uniforms, and clothes were always tough for me because I was growing so fast that I never had anything that fit well or looked good. The public school was much bigger than what I was used to. And the kids were different. I got into a lot of fights that first year. Maybe it was because I was the new kid or maybe because I was so big people wanted to test me. Whatever it was, I was fighting.

I had a fight in class once and got suspended. That was it for my mother. She sent me to live with my father.

It was cool living with my pops for a while. But I always had to be on my toes. I couldn't get away with anything. I never wanted to piss him off because I didn't want that strap, so I tried to stay out of trouble and stay out of his way.

As long as I did that, things were good. We would hang out like buddies. He could cook a little something, but we would go out to eat at different restaurants. He would take me hunting on the weekends. He introduced me to different music and really sparked a love of music in me. I loved to hear him sing. I enjoyed that.

He had a few rules—stay out of trouble and "make sure your behind is in the house when those streetlights come on. Don't let the dark catch you!"

I never did. I knew the consequences. He would go upside my head or put that strap to my butt, so I didn't want that. I got to hang out with him late if he was fixing the car. He would show me different things under the hood and how to change the oil and all of that. After a few weeks, though, I would start to miss my mom.

I would end up doing something to make him mad and he'd send me back to her. But he got it. After whipping my behind he would say, "I know you miss your mother, don't you?"

That was my thing. I knew what buttons to push to get back to my mom. But I would go back to my pops when I got to be too much for my mother. I was back and forth like that for about a year.

I wasn't a bad kid; I mostly got in trouble because I had to defend myself. I wasn't going to let anyone punk me, and if someone wanted to fight, I was going to give it to him.

Again, I had no perspective on my size. It must have looked crazy for me to be fighting kids my own age as big as I was. It couldn't be a fair fight. But since I didn't start the fights, I thought it was okay to finish them.

One teacher at my school noticed what was happening. He saw that some of the kids were getting kicks pushing my buttons and watching me go off. Mr. DiFillipio was my homeroom teacher and my science teacher, and he would give me assignments that would have me in the lab with him after classes. He took an interest in me, and if it wasn't for Mr. DiFillipio, I don't know what would have happened to me during those years. He taught me to believe in myself and that I mattered. Mr. DiFillipio made a huge difference in my life.

Unfortunately, Mr. DiFillipio wasn't there all the time. He couldn't save me from a lot of the bad things that were happening to me at home. But he was one bright spot in a whole lot of gray.

2) PERSONAL FOUL

My parents were a happy couple during the early parts of my growing up. A lot of laughter and partying went on in my home, and they always seemed to be going somewhere together.

My dad was a gospel singer. He had one of those old-style, booming gospel voices, and he would get booked a lot to sing at events and do church concerts on the weekends. My mom would be right there by his side.

They had different relatives babysit me while they went out. One of my relatives, I'll call him Paul, was about sixteen when he first babysat me. I was four or five. I was excited to have him babysit me because Paul was cool and I felt like a big man hanging with my older relative. That was before I was left alone with him.

That first night, before he put me to bed, everything changed. Paul said we were going to play this game. I liked to play. But the "game" he wanted me to play was not fun. It involved his touching me and his making me touch him and do things to him that back then I had no idea what I was doing. I just knew it was wrong.

I started crying. He told me to shut up and that if I told anyone, he would kill me. I believed him. Paul was my babysitter for a few years. I used to be happy to see my parents go out and have fun, but now I knew that meant that Paul would be coming over to watch me and my stomach would drop.

I used to talk to myself and tell myself that it wasn't so bad. That it was okay.

I mean it had to be okay because it kept happening to me. I thought maybe this was normal. When I used to stay at my grandmother's in the projects before we actually moved there, I had another relative, an older male, who played the same game with me. He was rougher and took it a little further than Paul. He used to hurt me and beat me. Again, he told me not to tell, or else.

I never told a soul what was going on.

I wish I could have told my mother. I really do. I could talk to my moms about almost anything, but this was one thing I just couldn't tell. By the time I had the courage to tell, I thought telling her would say something more about me. I mean, I allowed it to go on for so many years without saying anything. Maybe she would think that I liked it. Maybe she would think it was my fault.

Maybe I was sending them a signal, telling them that they could do that to me. At first, I didn't want to tell because I was scared. But then I didn't want to tell because I was afraid I might be looked at as being gay. I knew that I wasn't gay, but I didn't want that to even be out there like that.

And I didn't think anyone would believe me. I was known as a liar growing up, but that was because I was lying for my mother all the time. She would tell me to tell my father lies about what I needed—clothes, school supplies, whatever—so she could get more money from him. When they separated, my mother would send me to my father (when I wasn't staying with him) in old, bummy clothes or beat-down sneakers, knowing he would give me money to buy new clothes or shoes. The funny thing was, he knew her tricks. One time he pulled me aside and said, "Tell you mother if she needs something, she can just ask. Tell her to stop with the games."

He was no dummy. He also hated when we would only call when we needed something. He told me, "You can call to say hello sometime."

I got the message and I started calling him just to say hello.

"Hey, Pops, I just wanted to hear your voice," I would say. And we would end up talking for two hours. That was cool. But I still couldn't talk to him about what was happening with me. Many things I still couldn't tell him. Ever.

The other side of my pops was scary.

He wasn't a talker. He was no-nonsense. He was a screamer. When I got in trouble, it wasn't about no "time-outs." I would get whuppings or screamed on. Glass would shatter when he yelled. Usually the screaming came with the whupping. They went hand in hand. I never had to figure out *if* I was going to get a beating. I would wonder what he was going to beat me with—a belt, a switch, or something worse.

One day, I thought he was going to beat me to death. I was in the sixth grade at Public School 24 in Jersey City. I got suspended, probably for fighting. But my father had had enough of my getting in trouble.

He worked at the bus company cleaning buses. He brought home one of the hoses he used to rinse down the buses. This wasn't your average garden hose. This was one of those thick, dark green industrial hoses.

When my dad got home, he had something for me. That hose. He beat me everywhere with it, including over my head. Every time he hit me, I saw stars. I almost blacked out twice. I had lumps all over my head. My mother had to keep me out of school for two days after that beating.

At the time I wondered, *Is he trying to kill me?* I couldn't understand what I did to get that type of beating. If he felt that way about me, how could I ever tell him of the other kinds of beatings I was getting?

As I got older, I reflected on that time and wondered if he was beating me because he couldn't beat my mother. Was he taking out something more on me? I knew it couldn't be just my getting in trouble in school that made him *that* angry.

The next time I got suspended, I decided to hold off on that beating for a while. The principal said he wouldn't let me back in school until one of my parents came in. After that last beating, I wasn't telling anyone about this suspension. So for two months I would leave the house pretending to go to school. I knew eventually the gig would be up, but I was going to ride it out as long as I could.

My father's hours were eight to five, and my mother was in cosmetology school from nine in the morning to four thirty in the evening. So I would leave before my father and hang out until my mother left at nine. I would come back home and chill out for the rest of the day. One day, I was home chilling, watching television when the phone rang. My dumb ass answered it. It was my mother.

"What are you doing home?" she asked.

"I was suspended."

"When?"

"Two months ago."

She said the words I dreaded: "I'm going to tell your father."

He not only beat me at home, but he beat me in school and embarrassed the hell out of me. He slapped me in the face. (They would probably have locked him up had he beat me the way he did at home. He wasn't stupid.) I just stood there and took it. No way was I going to cry in front of my classmates. I waited until I went into the hallway, then let it go.

At the time I was really mad at my father. But over time, I grew to understand him. I grew to accept him. That was Pops. That's how he was raised, so he passed that along. Nobody said, "I love you," in his household.

He wasn't the affectionate type. I think I got maybe two hugs from my pops my whole life. Maybe it was more, I don't remember. But at least I have one of those hugs on film. After our first win over St. Anthony at home at the Dunn Sports Center in Elizabeth, my pops gave me a big bear hug. I still have the footage.

I know he did the best he knew how to do. But he was the last person I was going to talk to about being molested by my family members.

My mother I didn't tell for a different reason. I didn't want to burden her because I could see she was already going through some stuff. I was trying to protect her. She had so much other drama going on in her life at the time, I didn't want to add to it. I figured I could handle it. Things started going south with her and my dad around the time I was being regularly molested.

My mom was in what I called that crazy love. One moment she and my dad were cool, the next, we were moving out. They would get back to talking, then she would be crying and he would be crying and they would be back together. Then the next moment, we were back at my grandmother's. This went on for a few years until my mom finally moved on for good. But even then I was still going back and forth when it got too much for her. She would ship me off to stay with my father. But that wouldn't last.

I didn't really have anyone to confide in.

So I just started keeping everything inside, and when it got too much, I would act out. I would get into more fights, I would lie more, I would get into trouble.

In addition to that, I had trouble on the streets. After moving from my parents' home crosstown to my grandmother's apartment in the projects, I became a target. There were the bullies and clowns in school, and the hooligans and thugs in the neighborhood.

I used to get robbed coming home from school. I had a little crew I would walk home with, but the numbers would thin out a couple of blocks from my home. I would find myself walking alone by the time I made it to my block, a perfect target. The first time, these thugs looking for money roughed me up. The next time, they knew I didn't have money, so they took my shoes.

I went through some shit growing up, living in Jersey City. And I went through most of it by myself.

Looking back, I wish I had said something to somebody. I wish I had told because I know my mother would never have left me alone with him or anyone else.

I was scared. I was told that they would hurt my mother, that they would kill her. I didn't want to bring drama to the family. I was trying to save my family. I felt that if I didn't say anything, everything would be good. I was too young to understand. Why go through all of the fallout if I told? So I told myself to just deal with it. The way I dealt with it was to not talk. It became part of the routine of my life. It was just something that would happen that became part of my life and I just accepted it. I guess, to cope, I just blocked it out. I spent the majority of my life trying to cope on my own until I couldn't cope anymore.

I wish I had told, not just to protect me, but many others. Because people who do things like that to one kid usually do it to other kids. They don't stop at one. That other relative who used to rape me at my grandmother's is in jail. For rape. He raped his young niece.

I see Paul all the time. We don't speak about it, but he knows what he did, and he knows I know what he did. I want to confront him and talk it out with him. But instead, I've decided to forgive him. I had to let it go so that I can move on with my life.

Still, when I see him at family functions, because I do, it all comes back. I remember every detail. I look at him and I have to walk it off and go talk to God. That makes it better for me to deal with him.

I don't hold a grudge. In my heart, I talk to God. I ask Him to grant me the will to forgive. I'm still healing, and it's a stretch.

It's one of the hardest games I've ever had to play. But at least today I have someone to talk to about it. I have my wife, whom I can be totally honest with, who can talk me through the tough times. That's so important.

That is one of the most important lessons I can pass along to parents—make sure you allow your children to feel comfortable telling you anything. And watch the people you put in charge of them. Ask your child questions. If my mother had asked me if anyone had touched me, I would probably have said something then. She never asked. And I never told.

If parents want to make sure that their children aren't molested or messed with, they have to make it clear that their children can come and talk to them about *anything*—no matter what! I didn't feel that I could, so I didn't. And the molestation kept happening. And it wasn't just males.

A female family member molested me when I was nine. She was in high school. She also used to babysit me. When she did, she would bathe me and we started playing doctor. Again, I knew it was wrong. I knew it felt funny to be doing these things, but it was better than what my male cousins were doing to me. She wasn't rough the way they were. She wasn't hitting or beating me the way they were. It didn't feel as bad.

But it was still wrong. It was still molestation. It was still rape.

And still I couldn't tell anybody. So it was something

I kept inside, until nearly twenty years later when I met my wife and was able to let it all go.

Until then, my only savior was basketball.

On the courts, I wasn't being molested, or teased. I wasn't weird or a freak. I wasn't too big. My feet weren't too big. My clothes weren't out of style. I wasn't out of place.

I was the man on the basketball courts. I was somebody. People liked me and wanted to be around me because I played basketball. I found some place where I fit in, where I could forget the horrible things.

I found the same escape in music. I could get lost in the beats, in the melodies. I could find strength in the lyrics. When mixing one record with the next, I could make the crowd move. I could be in control of everything. People loved me when I took the turntables, when I played the guitar or drums, when I sang. I was special.

Thank God for music and basketball.

3) HOOP DREAMS

Moving to the projects was one of the worst transitions for me. I wasn't a street kid. My mother had me in church most of my youth, and I was in Catholic school through the fifth grade. When my parents split, money was tight and I had to go to public school. I not only had to go to public school, but in a neighborhood where I had no friends. So I spent most of my days in the house. When I wasn't in the house, I was in school or in my neighborhood getting into fights.

I spent a lot of my time in my grandmother's room at the back of her first-floor apartment. She didn't have any bars on the windows because people in the neighborhood knew her and they also knew she was packing pistols. That was all the security she needed.

Her room overlooked the playground in back of the Booker T. Washington projects on Freemont Street. I would sit in her window and watch as the kids gathered around after school and played. The action on the basketball courts looked like so much fun.

The kids playing ball and the whole atmosphere seemed so different from what I'd experienced since moving here. Rough. That was the only description of that neighborhood. Some sort of fight always seemed to be breaking out, with a lot of drug use and drug dealing. But the basketball courts seemed like a safe haven.

I sat watching from my grandmother's window for months until I worked up the courage to go out there and play. I was nearly six feet tall at age ten and had never picked up a basketball. I was awkward and didn't know how to dribble or shoot well, but I was hooked.

By the summer, I would wake up, take a bath or wash up, and be out there playing all day. It was natural. I wanted to do stuff to stay out of trouble. I wanted to do things to stay out of fights. The courts seemed like the safest place.

We played 21, Taps, and Respect. Respect was just shooting around. If you made it, you got the ball back; if you didn't, you had to give it up. There was no score in Respect, but I got to work on my shot.

Some of the kids played in a summer tournament, and one of the coaches who lived in my grandmother's building and saw me out there trying to play asked me if I wanted to play in the next tournament. I said yeah. So he put me in the mix.

My first game I played with the Biddies. They should have called it the Biddies plus a Biggie because I was the tallest kid out there. On one of the first plays, I blocked a shot by my teammates, got the rebound, and scored a basket for the other team. It was funny. But thank goodness, we didn't lose the game. I would probably have got jumped.

My basketball playing went to another level when school began. This kid Terry Dehere went to St. Patrick's, my old Catholic school on Bramhall Avenue in Jersey City. When I moved, I was back and forth from my old neighborhood to the new one because my parents would shuffle me back and forth when I got in trouble. When I stayed with my dad, I had to walk across town to school. My dad lived on Oxford Avenue on the west side of Jersey City between Kennedy Boulevard and West Side Avenue. My mom was at Booker T. Washington before we moved to Irvington.

When I would walk from Booker T. to Public School 24, which was crosstown, I would often see Terry walking to school. He stopped me one day and asked me if I wanted to play on this basketball team. I said sure. He gave me the information, and that week I showed up to practice for the Catholic Youth Organization in Jersey City. Terry and I were the stars on that CYO team.

While I didn't have many offensive skills, I was a

natural on defense. Blocking shots came easily. Being tall helps with that. Any ball that came toward the basket, I could jump up and slap it away. I was also good at rebounding. Again, just being tall gave me an advantage. I was already up there near the basket. I didn't know anything about boxing out back then, but it didn't matter. I could jump.

My sheer size intimidated most of my opponents. I loved that reaction. I loved making people think before shooting a layup or a shot near the basket with me around. I learned that basketball was as much about the mental as it was about the physical. I could take people out of their game without blocking every shot. They would be messed up just thinking that I might or that I could.

The year after Terry left for high school, I stayed on our CYO team and we won a city championship. I was in the eighth grade and was starting to get noticed.

That summer, I was getting ready for high school. It was a big deal and everybody was telling me I should go to St. Anthony in Jersey City. Everybody in the hood was telling me to go there. That was the best basketball team in the state and one of the best in the country. I didn't have a clue.

Mr. DiFillipio was there for me again. We were doing some one-on-one tutoring, getting me ready for high school, and I asked him what he thought I should do. He said I should go to St. Anthony. He said if I was serious about basketball, going there would definitely take me far.

Coach Bobby Hurley called my moms and talked to me about going there, and that September I was a member of state champion St. Anthony.

The summer before I went to St. Anthony, my mom got remarried.

Since the split between my mother and my father, my mother was real careful about bringing men around. She never had a boyfriend, not that I knew of. She never brought any men around us talking about "This is uncle so-and-so." The first man she brought around was Numa. But Numa had always been there. He was a friend of the family. So when she told me they were getting married, I was surprised, but he wasn't a stranger.

That summer, they got married in our living room. I wasn't happy about it. I was holding out hope that she and my father would get back together. But I could see that my mother was happy. This scrawny, skinny man loved my mother. He was a good guy. So I had to let it go.

That summer we moved from the projects to a house in Irvington. I finally got a chance to have my own space again. I was happy to be leaving Booker T. behind.

The only thing I missed about being at my grandmother's was the cooking. My moms could throw down. But grandma was the queen of the kitchen. You could smell her food from way down the hall. She was sick with the hoecakes. She made the best soul food I have ever had in my life. I really missed her cooking. But I didn't miss her soap operas.

With Numa, I also appreciated having another father figure—after I got to know him.

Numa taught me to stand up straight. Being the tallest in every class, I got into the habit of slouching. I didn't want to be big. But he told me to stand up straight and tall. Numa did the little things for me that mattered. My daddy put those things in me, but Numa brought them out. Numa also came to all of my basketball games and did other things with us.

He was Haitian and used to take us to the West Indian Day Parade along Eastern Parkway in Brooklyn. In the summers, he would take us to the beach and on picnics. We would also go to a pool in north Jersey. We did a lot of fun stuff with "Poppi," which is what we called Numa.

Numa had kids from his first wife and would sometimes have his kids with us when we took our family trips. One of his sons, Ricky, even moved in with us. So we were one big happy family.

Ricky and I played AAU basketball together. I took him to the NBA with me when I first moved out to Utah. He was like my personal assistant. Most players have their people with them. They have their boys or family members work for them. LeBron James has his whole crew from high school working for him. Lamar Odom has his uncle as his driver. You need your support system. Ricky was there for me. He was one of my best friends.

• • •

When I enrolled in St. Anthony, I was reunited with Terry Dehere. I was playing with Bobby Hurley Jr. and Jerry Walker, one of the best guards and forwards in the state. I knew them from summer-league play and AAU basketball. But if you knew anything about New Jersey basketball during this time, Terry Dehere, Bobby Hurley, and Jerry Walker were household names.

That year, St. Anthony was one of the best basketball schools in the nation. Terry, Jerry, and Bobby all ended up in the pros. That was one special team. I don't think there's been another high school team with so much firepower. They were so talented that I never really got to play with them. I couldn't crack the varsity.

Coming from Jersey and being a baller, everybody wanted to go to St. Anthony. That school was like North Carolina or Duke or UCLA back in the day.

St. Anthony was a Catholic school and it cost money to go there. My family couldn't afford it, but Mr. Hurley pulled some strings and got me in. I got a scholarship that paid for most of my tuition, but my mom and pops still had to kick in some money that they didn't have. But I was starting to see that basketball could pay off. I was getting an opportunity to go to one of the best schools in the state for almost free because I could play a sport.

I was excited to be playing for one of the best teams in the country. But moving to Irvington made the commute a challenge. It was a long way away from Jersey City, and I had to take a couple of buses and a train and then walk several blocks to get to school every day. It was a two-hour commute on a good day, which meant I had to get up super-early to get to school and with practice or a late game wouldn't get home some nights until after ten.

I was having a hard time getting to school on time and would miss a class or two most weeks, which got me in trouble. While the basketball team was favored at St. Anthony, the nuns definitely weren't fans of Lou Bee (my nickname). They didn't care that I was a basketball player. All they cared about were my academics, and I wasn't doing so well in that area.

Mr. Hurley started letting me stay over at his house. The Hurleys lived in Country Village in a town house. It was bigger than my house in Irvington, and it was cool staying with them on game nights and after some late practices. But it still wasn't helping with my classes. I was struggling.

Mr. Hurley had me playing with the varsity team during practices but kept me on the junior varsity for the games. I didn't get any burn that season. He didn't think I was ready for prime time, I guess. But I was hanging with Terry, Jerry, and Bobby in practice.

Mr. Hurley was the first coach who really yelled at me. He was tough. He was definitely a winning coach. But his style didn't help me get better. I didn't do well when people yelled at me.

I ended up flunking out of St. Anthony.

During the season, at the suggestion of Mr. Hurley, I joined the New Jersey Roadrunners, Jersey's AAU team, one of the best in the nation, and another door opened.

4) SANDY

met Sandy Pyonin at an AAU tryout in Plainfield, New Jersey. I didn't know who Sandy was before I met him. I'd never heard of him. But he was legendary on the AAU circuit. He has probably won more AAU championships than anyone else in the history of New Jersey. And he's still winning.

Coach Hurley told me about him. When I first got to St. Anthony, Hurley told me I should think about trying out for Sandy's team. But it wasn't a typical tryout. If Sandy asked you to try out, you pretty much made the team. Bobby, Terry, Jerry, and I "tried out," but it was understood that we would be on the team.

I was the youngest kid on the team, but I was probably the biggest player Sandy ever coached. I was about six-seven and everybody wanted me on his team. Every coach thought he could win with me. But Sandy saw more in me. He was already a winner. He didn't need me to win. In addition to Bobby, Terry, and Jerry, our team also featured Waliyy Dixon, this highflier from Linden, who ended up making a name for himself on one of those AND1 teams—the street-basketball league, which was a blend of hip-hop, the Harlem Globetrotters, WWE, and the NBA. They called Waliyy "the Main Event" because he could jump out of the building and do some off-the-chain dunks.

I didn't know enough to be scared or intimidated playing on this team. I remember walking into the gym for the first tryout and I was playing against Anthony Avent from Shabazz High in Newark, who ended up being the *Star-Ledger* player of the year, and Alaa Abdelnaby, this six-ten dude from Bloomfield High, who ended up playing for Duke and going on to a pretty decent NBA career.

I saw basketball being played as I had never seen it played before. It seemed as if everybody could dunk and block shots. I wasn't special. I'd never saw anyone shoot three-pointers like that or play run-and-gun basketball. The level of competition was higher than I had ever seen. I was this kid playing against and with players who might as well be professionals.

Then I saw Sandy. He seemed totally out of place. I was thinking, *What does this short, scrawny, curly-haired dude know about basketball?*

But in that first afternoon, I saw that he knew a lot. Sandy had a system. He wasn't this guy who had a bunch of great players and let them do what they wanted. He had a vision and a plan and he implemented that plan. And as good as they all were physically, he made them better ballplayers.

With me, he concentrated on ball-handling drills, shooting drills, dunking drills, things I had never before done. I ran sprints and lifted weights. I hated it. I liked to play basketball but I hated to practice. I just wanted to play. Some days I wanted to quit. Those drills were not fun—especially the suicides and all of that working out.

But Sandy wouldn't let me quit. He had his tactics. He knew what buttons to push to make me keep going.

"Well, Lou, if you don't run these suicides, we're not going to get anything to eat," he would say.

He knew the way to this man's heart was through my stomach. That was motivation.

"If you don't finish these drills, you won't get those sneakers you want."

I would work out hard because I wanted those new sneakers. Sure, it was bribery, but it worked. Sandy didn't have to yell and scream to get us to do things. He was just cool, and after a while we wanted to work hard for him. He would also take us to the movies, to the beach, or out to eat. He was there for all of us. Sandy was my friend as well as my coach. Still is.

I knew Sandy cared about me beyond basketball.

Knowing that made it easier for me to stick around and work harder than I wanted to. I didn't want to let him down. The relationship I had with Sandy was different from any other coach. He was an extended-parent-type figure. He checked in on me every day. He was a good guy.

Sandy took an instant liking to me. He saw my potential—and it wasn't just my height. He saw where I could be. He saw I could be as good as Wilt Chamberlain, Bill Russell, and Kareem Abdul-Jabbar. He taught me how to not just use my size, but about finesse and how to move without the ball and shoot.

He really worked on my game. But I still had other kinks to work out inside.

The molestation, which I'd tried to put out of my mind, would creep up in different ways. It was like an invisible chain around my neck weighing me down. I hated showering with other kids. On basketball teams, it wasn't unusual for kids to shower after their games before heading home. In fact, it was the norm. I'm sure they must have looked at me as one nasty dude, but I wouldn't shower.

Sandy had his rules. He wanted us to shower after games. I guess he didn't want to ride around with a bunch of funky kids in his car, and I don't blame him. But I wouldn't shower.

We had a game at the Meadowlands once. It was a big deal. I somehow knew I wouldn't be able to get out of taking a shower there, so I drank a whole bottle of Vicks Formula 44. I tried to make myself sick so I wouldn't have to play in the game and take a shower later. It worked. I missed the game.

For me, the shower meant I would have to be naked. I didn't want to be naked in front of anyone. I felt too vulnerable. I felt too out of control.

Sandy had no idea what was going on with me (or maybe he did). But he never pressed the issue. He was real good with handling me. He focused on my game and dangling the things I wanted—new gear, sneakers, going to the movies, going out to eat, etc.—and that helped me in other areas.

Sandy immersed me in basketball. He wanted me to get the jump hook down like Kareem. He wanted me to rebound like Wilt Chamberlain, Bob Lanier, and Jack Sikma. Be versatile like Bill Russell. He sat me down and made me watch films of these guys. I didn't really appreciate it then. I didn't even know who many of them were. I didn't understand all the hype. When you're young and have no perspective on the world, you can't see any further than where you are. But I sat there and watched because I knew I would be getting some pizza afterward.

Flunking out of St. Anthony was humbling. I wanted to prove that I wasn't a dummy. Sandy wasn't mad at me for flunking out. Instead he was committed to making sure I was prepared for the following year. That summer he got me a tutor and had me go to summer school at his school, Solomon Schechter Day School of Essex and Union in West Orange. I didn't quite fit in. It was a Jewish school, but Sandy picked me up and dropped me off every day and made sure I was getting the work done.

I passed every test I had to take that summer.

I was in school every day from nine in the morning until noon, then I would be on the basketball courts from one until it got dark. When I look back on it now, that was a great summer. I got a lot done. I was able to get up to speed in the classroom, and my basketball game went to the next level.

Sandy had it down to a science. He had our workouts written down. I didn't see the plan or the vision, but it all came together. He was persistent and consistent, but he also had compassion. He would drop me off at night after a day of practice and play, and he would tell me he would pick me up the next morning. And he did.

I wanted to hang with my boys and not play ball. But he made sure I stayed on top of my studies and stayed in the gym and molded me into this nationally recognized phenom that every college in the country wanted on its team. Sandy did that. His commitment to me made that happen. I was his project and he found a way to get the most out of me—on the court and off. Sandy also made sure I stayed out of trouble. He kept me so busy that I didn't have time for much else. It was just basketball and school, AAU tournaments, and traveling. I was the main attraction.

I worked hard so that I was eligible to play my sophomore year. I did the work. Nothing illegal was done, no strings were pulled.

Sandy was instrumental in getting me serious about basketball. He wanted me to be one of the best to ever play the game.

That summer, the New Jersey Roadrunners went to the National Tournament in Florida. I had a ball. I got to see something outside of my neighborhood and to play with some of the best in the country.

Had Sandy not come along, I would probably be a seven-foot-two-inch crossing guard or mailman or bagger at Pathmark.

He had a lot to do with my becoming a household name.

5) PLEASE DON'T STOP
THE MUSIC

Colonel Abrams was not going to let you get the best of him. Barbara Tucker was taking it deep, deep inside, deep, deep down inside. There was Crystal Waters and her "Gypsy Woman" ("La da dee, la dee da . . ."). *The password is Nu-Nu.* And there was CeCe Peniston with those sick vocals over that beat. *Finally!*

I was officially in love with house music.

Jersey City wasn't really up on house or club music. The people were mainly into disco, R&B, and hip-hop. But when I moved to Irvington, my world opened up. All I heard along the streets of Irvington and Newark, blasting from cars and homes, was house music.

At first I thought, *Man, these people are corny with that.* But the more I heard, the more I got it. And the more I loved it.

House music, all night long, drove Newark and Irvington. That beat made everything move.

I made a friend in the neighborhood, Kevin. He had turntables and a mixer set up in his basement. He was a deejay and would let me come listen to him for hours on end that summer. He even showed me how to deejay. I was hooked. I would go over there every day.

I was just getting into this basketball thing, but music had always been my first love. It was one of the bonds that tied my dad and me together, and it definitely helped me get through some rough times. Now it was being taken to a whole new level with turntables and mixing, experimenting with beats and different kinds of music.

I was raised in a musical home. My dad was always in some kind of singing group, and my mom was always throwing a party. Our home had music flowing through it all of the time. It was mostly gospel—the Mighty Clouds of Joy and Aretha Franklin (early, old-school church Aretha before she crossed over to R&B). But Moms also loved the blues, and she loved her some Sam Cooke, Otis Redding, and James Brown. So I loved them, too.

My father bought me a set of drums when I was

about nine because he got tired of hearing me bang on the pots and pans in the house. I never had a lesson. I just always had this thing for sounds and music. I was good. My father bought me my first guitar when I was ten. I had been playing around with the guitar in church. One of the band members showed me some chords and I just picked it up.

I couldn't read music and I never had a guitar lesson, but if you showed me something, I could just pick it up. Or if I heard it two or three times, I could usually do it. I have a gifted ear when it comes to music.

I was playing in bands from an early age—playing the drums and guitar and even singing. But the summer where I learned to mix records in my man Kevin's basement changed my musical world forever.

I asked Sandy to get me some turntables. Of course, he bribed me to work out extra hard for a week and I did. He then took me to an electronics store and I picked out these Technics 1200 and a Genesis mixer. I had a little vinyl collection, but I started buying twelve-inches like crazy. By the end of the summer, I had two crates of records full of a little bit of everything, but mostly house.

I would set up my turntables outside—snaking an extension cord outside my window—and play for the neighborhood.

I started going to clubs a little later. When I got to high school, my boys and I would be at a club just about every Friday and Saturday. They were there to talk to the girlies. I did that, too. But I was mostly there listening to the deejays and picking up pointers and stealing song sequences.

"Jack Your Body" by J. M. Silk mixed with Marshall Jefferson's "Move Your Body (House Music Anthem)" was a sure hit. But every deejay had different ways of mixing, and I loved seeing the different ways people could take the same music and make magic and get the crowd to scream or ooh and aah. One deejay would take out the bass and rock the crowd. Another would take out the treble and just have that bass grinding, and that would drive the crowd wild—the way I went wild the first time I heard "Black Betty," the club version.

I loved that—moving the crowd, seeing them worked into a frenzy by throwing one song on after another. It wasn't just the song, but the deejay's way that he did his thing. I couldn't stand deejays that talked over the music or had hype men talking over the music. If you were really good, you didn't need that. You just needed to know how to feel that music and what to do to make the crowd holler. I respected deejays that did their work with their hands.

Funkmaster Flex at the Tunnel in Manhattan, where you found a little bit of everything from B-boys breaking to dudes voguing on the top level. There was DJ Scratch. If Tony Humphries was deejaying somewhere, I was there. I would go see Kid Capri wherever he was playing live in my area. He put on a show that was as good as a concert.

Man, those dudes were so creative. I would be in my own world, smoking an el and watching these deejays do their thing. I was listening for that one song—that one song that would make the crowd go bananas, and I was going to get it the next day if I didn't already have it. I wanted to get that same reaction the next time I deejayed.

When I became Luther Wright, basketball star, I used to get into the clubs for free. I could even go into the deejay booth and they would let me spin for a set or two. I was getting a reputation for being good on the turntables.

I used to spin at Sensations a lot. I didn't have a deejay job, but when I would roll through, I would do guest spots every now and then. I was known as a basketball player, but I wanted to be known just as much as a good deejay.

Club Zanzibar on Broad Street in Newark next to the Lincoln Motel was the mecca for club music back in the day. Zanzibar, to this day, is legendary. If you were into club music, you knew about Club Zanzibar. I never made it to the deejay booth of the third floor, where the hard-core house music was played. It was serious and nobody was giving up a minute on the turntables there. But I was able to spin for about an hour on the second floor, and I was in heaven.

If you could rock a crowd at Club Zanzibar—no matter what floor—you were the shit. And that night, I was the shit.

Seeing the crowd go wild when I put on *that* song is a feeling I cannot describe. I guess that's what I loved so much about basketball. Making people feel something based on something I did. If I got a hard rebound, blocked someone's shot across the gym, or dunked on somebody, the crowd would ooh and aah. I loved to hear that.

The equivalent to Club Zanzibar in basketball was the Rucker up in Harlem. The Rucker was *the* place to ball in the country. Everybody—from NBA players to legendary street ballers—would show up to these courts to show out. It didn't matter who you were, you could get embarrassed if you didn't come correct at the Rucker.

It wasn't just about playing against the best of the best in the world. It was the crowd. They were part of the game. They let you know when you did something great, and they let you know when you didn't.

It was like *Showtime at the Apollo* for basketball. I craved that instant reaction. I guess it's why I couldn't stand it when I got benched or when I didn't get to play, because the biggest part of basketball or music for me was the people. It was the love I got from them.

6) ELIZABETH, I'M COMING TO JOIN YOU!

heard people comparing me to Shaquille O'Neal. They were saying I'd be the player that would compete against him in the NBA. It would be Bill Russell and Wilt Chamberlain all over again. But I didn't understand what that meant. I didn't see it for myself, so I couldn't possibly live up to that.

But Sandy saw it. When I flunked out of St. Anthony, he had a plan for me. Elizabeth High School.

I didn't know much about Elizabeth High School in Elizabeth, New Jersey. But one of the first things I learned my first day of school was that it was the largest school in America. It was definitely the largest school

I had ever seen. That first day was like "Wow!" It was jaw-dropping seeing a building that big. Elizabeth High sat on a whole city block. The campus was humongous. More than a thousand students were in my graduating class.

Seeing all of those kids was overwhelming. It was impossible to know everybody. It seemed as if I were meeting new people every day for three years.

The first day of school, I missed three classes in a row because I couldn't find my class. That's how big the campus was. I looked at my schedule and went to the class that I thought was written on my schedule. I felt as if I were walking in circles. I finally went over to a security guard and he asked me, "What house is your class in?" *What house?* I had no idea what he was talking about. He told me I had the right class number, but I was in the wrong *building* or house. I didn't realize that Elizabeth was made up of two buildings—Halsey and Dwyer. That's how big the school was. That was an adjustment.

Unless you had lunch, or a free period, you had to get out of class and boogie to the next class, which could be in the other building. It was like walking from Thirty-third Street to Thirty-seventh Street in Manhattan. If you stopped to say hello or get a hug from your girl, or even to go to the bathroom, you would definitely be late.

So there was no hanging in the hallways at Elizabeth. When that bell rang, it was as if a subway car had let out during rush hour in Queens. And you couldn't get away with an excuse if you were late. Teachers at Elizabeth didn't play that. If you were late, you would get detention. I never got detention, though. I was Lou Bee.

The first week of school a student protest was held outside. I had never seen a protest like that before except on television, where I had seen people strike and hold picket signs and stuff like that. But I had never seen kids involved in anything like this.

Elizabeth students were protesting about teacher pay or more rights for teachers or something the Board of Education had done. The football team was leading the protest. They had signs and were yelling, but it didn't get out of hand, which was surprising considering how many kids there were. Whatever it was they were standing up for, you could see the passion. The students were passionate about a lot of things at Elizabeth High.

"Iron" Mike Tyson came to speak at the school. He was at the height of his career and it was a big deal. As he made his way to the podium, the students bum-rushed him. The kids wanted to just touch him, he was so popular at this time. He wasn't as big as I expected him to be physically, but he was huge to me.

Mike Tyson had knocked out a bunch of dudes, was heavyweight champion of the world, but he was no match for the student body at Elizabeth High School. Security had to protect Mike Tyson, and they ushered him out of there. He didn't even get to say hello or

"This is ludicrous" or anything. He had to scamper out of there.

I felt that we students had power at Elizabeth High. Going to this school was going to be interesting.

The commute was a big change from going to St. Anthony, with that two-hour trip. While I didn't live in the town, it wasn't that far from Irvington—just one bus ride away. Some days, I would catch a ride with another teammate, Chris Gatlin, who also lived in Irvington. His dad would pick me up.

I got into Elizabeth the way most athletes who lived in another city ended up playing for major teams in New Jersey (and probably everywhere else)—somebody hooked me up with an address. My report card and all school reports went to an address on Anna Street in Elizabeth. I never lived there and never even visited. But that's how things were done.

Going to Elizabeth wasn't just great for me for basketball. It was also great culturally.

Elizabeth High was a true melting pot. There were the Mexicans, the Puerto Ricans, the Cubans, the Jamaicans, the white people, the Dominicans, and the Haitians. You had this group fighting that one. This one hanging with that one. It was crazy.

But I never had any problems. While everybody was fighting everybody else, they were all loving me. It didn't take long for people to figure out that I would be a major figure in Elizabeth High School history. The school was mostly known for football and baseball. But

I put them on the map with basketball. They had never had a seven-foot-two-inch dominant center like me. I was literally big man on campus. I was the Obama of Elizabeth High.

This was the first time in my life that I loved going to school. It was definitely something to get up in the morning and be excited about going to school. Can you imagine that? The fun was happening even before I picked up a ball for the school.

I hung out with the popular crowd. We were the BMOCs. We even had the cafeteria on lock. Everyone wanted to sit in our section, but you had to have a pass to sit with us. It wasn't a physical pass; it was an unspoken pass. You needed to be on the football team, the baseball team, the basketball team, or you needed to be popular.

I also hung out with big-time drug dealers in high school because they always had cars and money and the hookup. They used to take me to the clubs in New York and we would party all weekend. I didn't realize how much danger I was putting myself in at the time. I was a kid having fun. And I got all the free weed I wanted. It was in high school when I really started smoking.

I had my first drink of alcohol when I was at St. Anthony. At a party at the local boys' club they were passing a bottle in a paper bag. The bottle got passed to me and I hesitated.

"If you don't drink this, Lou Bee, you can't hang with us," one of my boys said.

"Word?" I said, taking the bottle and taking a swig.

It was real nasty. I started coughing and making faces.

"What's that?" I asked.

Everyone fell out laughing. It was Boone's Farm or Mad Dog 20/20 or something like that. Just nasty!

It tasted nothing like the Pink Champale my mother used to drink. I used to sneak sips from her cup during the house parties she would throw from time to time. I was eight years old and thought I was doing something. She left her cup on the table and left the room for something. I sneaked over and took her cup and took a sip. It was both sweet and bitter going down and it made my entire chest warm. I felt like a grown-up. I felt even better because I didn't get caught.

But that hard, cheap liquor they were drinking at this boys' club party wasn't for me. I never took to drinking much. I only drank when I was at a party and everyone else was drinking. People would buy drinks for me later on after I was a pro and even after I left the league. Later, when I became a heavy drug user, I would only drink when I ran out of drugs or couldn't get drugs. Liquor was my last drug of choice, but it would do in a pinch to take the edge off when I needed it.

At Elizabeth High I discovered weed. And that became my thing . . . until basketball season started.

Basketball changed everything. While I was popular and the man before basketball season even started, when the season did start, it was nuts. Elizabeth High had never seen anything like me. And I had never seen anything like it. The number of students showing up for our games made it feel as if I were playing for the Knicks in Madison Square Garden. They had pep rallies, bands, cheerleaders—all for us.

Playing for Coach Candelino was another plus. He had the perfect style for me. He was tough and demanding, but cool.

He had an open-door policy. I could sit and talk to him about anything. We would talk about sports, his family, my family—he would just shoot it with me. We had a great relationship. It wasn't like "I'm the coach, and you're the player."

He treated us as if we were his kids. He wasn't as concerned with the Ws and Ls as he was with me as a person. He would call and check in on my moms from time to time, too.

Coming in, though, I had a little issue with Candelino, or rather, he had an issue with me and I thought we were going to have some problems. He wasn't really feeling the celebrity I came into the school with. But after that first practice, he saw how my celebrity status would help his team.

During the early recruiting period, we would have some of the biggest coaches in the nation—Rollie Massimino from Villanova, Jerry Tarkanian from University of Nevada–Las Vegas (UNLV), Rick Pitino, who had just come to Kentucky that year in 1989, Jim Boeheim from Syracuse, and P. J. Carlesimo from Seton Hall, as well as a few other Division I coaches—lined up around our gym and in the bleachers watching our practices.

Coach Candelino discovered that even though the coaches were there to see me, the other players on my team were getting a look, too—a look they might not have got otherwise. Quite a few got scholarships. Mike Brennan ended up at Princeton; Lawrence Thomas got a scholarship to go to Farleigh Dickinson. Isaac Morgan ended up at Farleigh Dickinson, and Malik Jackson went to Rutgers.

That first year, I averaged more than seventeen points, ten rebounds, and three blocks, and just about every college in the nation wanted me to play for them.

One of the highlights of that year was our game against Linden. They were our biggest rivals in the country—them and St. Anthony, of course. But Linden was in our division and they always had good players. They beat us my first year on the team. I sat out most of that game with back spasms. I still thought we should have won. I hated to lose. I was on a mission to tear a chunk out their asses the next time we met.

Linden didn't beat us another game—not as long as I was on the team. The next time we met, it was payback time. I had about twenty points and twelve rebounds, and when that final buzzer rang, I remember feeling vindicated.

I was All-State in New Jersey that year. I didn't make the first team All-American. (I was third team.) But I considered myself the No. 1 player in New Jersey.

I was definitely the most highly recruited basketball player in the state.

The only other team getting more recognition than Elizabeth High School or who had players that were also highly recruited was St. Anthony of Jersey City. I couldn't seem to shake them. New Jersey had a Tournament of Champions that year, a kind of high school Final Four that pitted the best four teams in the state—both Catholic schools and publics—against one another.

We played them twice that year. The first time was a blur. I had the flu, I was out of it, and we got blown out. The second time we played them was in the Tournament of Champions for all the marbles.

It was a close game. But St. Anthony had this thing with them that they couldn't lose. They were undefeated that year. And while I think we only lost by six, I could tell they weren't worried. Bobby, Terry, and Jerry kicked our butts. They were the best team in New Jersey that year. They were the best team in the country, ranked No. 1. But that team may have been the best high school team in the history of the state.

The next year, I was on a mission. There would be no excuses. It was my senior year, and Bobby, Terry, and Jerry had all graduated. In our first meeting against St. Anthony we destroyed them. It was never close. They didn't have a chance. They scored the first two points of that game, but that was it. We went on a tear and they never had a chance.

My team was talented and we knew how to win.

Elizabeth was supposed to win, with our team. It was expected. But I still couldn't help crying. I was crying for all of the games that I didn't get to play in at St. Anthony. I was crying about all of the stuff that was said about me and how I couldn't live up to the hype. I was crying because I knew I was leaving high school a winner. I was crying for all of it.

Some of the St. Anthony players were crying, too, for different reasons.

Three years of tears had built up for me, and I just let them all go after that game. So much was behind those tears. It wasn't just the win.

To beat them was a dream come true. When I left St. Anthony, the sisters didn't think I would pan out. They didn't tell me to my face, but I heard things. They felt that I would never amount to anything if I didn't play at St. Anthony, that I would never play on the same level.

Part of those tears was vindication. It was proving them wrong. Who were they to say just because I didn't play at their school that I wouldn't be shit? I spent the next three years proving them wrong. With the help of Sandy Pyonin and Coach Candelino, I didn't just hang with St. Anthony, I beat them.

You can never say what someone's going to be or not going to be. You can never limit any person. God's got the final word. It doesn't matter what man says. It only matters what God says.

After we won the state championship, we were taken to city hall to meet the mayor. They named a day after us. They made mugs with our team picture on them. We won three straight state public-school championships and one Tournament of Champions. That was the highlight. They acknowledged us with jackets, too. We were celebrities in Elizabeth and it felt good.

A pizza parlor was across from the high school. Every time I went there, the owner would treat me to whatever I wanted. I liked that feeling. It was just a taste of what was to come.

7) DECISION TIME

The first letter from a college came for me in the eighth grade when I was at Public School 41. The package had a Fighting Irish shield on the envelope, and it included a program from the basketball team with players' and coaches' bios. It was from this school called Notre Dame. I had never heard of them before, but they'd heard of me. They sent me a letter, inviting me to come to their school on a full scholarship. I was only thirteen years old!

I didn't understand or appreciate what that meant, and looking back, I wish I had saved some of those letters that started coming steadily when I was at P.S. 41.

After I got that first letter, it seemed as though one came every week. All wanted me to play for them or try out for their AAU team. I was six feet eight and a half inches in the eighth grade, and while I wasn't as good as I would later become, my height seemed to be enough.

One of the biggest decisions I had to make during high school was where I was going to go to college. I was the most sought-after player in New Jersey at the time. All were telling me I should go to their school and that they were the best for me, that they would make me a star. Before basketball season started in my senior year, I got to visit a few schools that I was considering.

I went to the University of Kentucky on a visit because of Rick Pitino. I liked his style and he was a winner. He'd won at a little school, Providence, before going to Kentucky. He was selling me on their tradition and his winning ways. Kentucky was a big basketball school with one of the premier programs in the country.

He personally showed me around campus. He took me to the gym, and when I came in, he had me go through the tunnel. The lights were out, and as I walked through, a spotlight came on me and over the loudspeaker I heard, "And starting at center for your Kentucky Wildcats . . . Luuuuuuuuuuther Wright!"

That was cool. I liked that.

Pitino was in the midst of rebuilding, coming out of a scandal at Kentucky. An investigation found the school guilty of several NCAA violations, including money paid to a player by one of the assistant coaches under head coach Eddie Sutton, and another player given help on his college entrance exams. Kentucky was banned from NCAA competition and was almost given the "death penalty," which would have shut down the whole basketball program for two years. Instead they were banned from television play (which is huge money and exposure for any school) for two years from 1988 to 1989.

Pitino was brought in to restore order and respectability. He had just done his thing at Providence and was looked at as the savior of Kentucky. He wanted me to be a part of his rebuilding. He kept it real. He told me that the school was under a lot of NCAA scrutiny and was walking on eggshells, but he wanted me to be a part of what he was building. I felt I could play with Pitino and be productive. But it was Kentucky. That was a long way from Jersey. It was just too far.

I also visited Syracuse before my senior season started. This school felt like home. My visit there was like one big slumber party. Derrick Coleman was their star, and someone whom I really looked up to. We had a lot in common. He was a big guy, like me, and just a down-to-earth city boy, also like me. He was my idol.

I felt that I could be myself at Syracuse and I could really see myself playing there. I would have been able to step right in because I would have had Derrick Coleman as my mentor. He was already taking me under his wing.

They rolled out the red carpet for me at Syracuse. They took me to eat at a nice restaurant. They introduced me to some of their boosters. I got to go to the Carrier Dome. There is really no other place like it in college basketball. Actually, there aren't too many pro arenas as big and as loud as the Carrier Dome.

I had a blast on my visit and I really liked the way they supported their athletes at Syracuse. The student body was off the hook. They expected to win every game because the "'Cuse was in the house." Oh my God!

That year, they went on to the NCAA championships and lost to Indiana in the finals. I knew I could help them get that championship. I wanted to win one with Syracuse. I really felt that I could fit in there. And I had known head coach Jim Boeheim for a long time. He had been following me for a few years now and I thought he was a nice guy.

After that visit, I made up my mind. I was going to be an Orangeman.

But I had one problem—my mother. Her health was bad and getting worse. When I got to Elizabeth High, my mom started getting sick. She had a bunch of health issues—she had her gallbladder removed, she was diagnosed with an enlarged heart, and she had diabetes. By my junior year, she had to get a pacemaker.

One time before she got the pacemaker, we had a real scare. She had just got a big-screen television, and we were sitting around watching it and enjoying some show together and she was talking to me. All of a sudden she just passed out in my lap. Her heart went out.

You can't imagine how it feels to hold your mother in your arms, not knowing if she's going to make it. It was crazy. I called the ambulance and the hospital kept her for about a month.

I was worried that I might lose my mom. All I was thinking was "Not right now. Don't leave me now." That's Ma-Dukes. You only get one of those. After practice I would head to Beth Israel. I would go back and forth every day to Beth Israel Hospital to see her. That's when they gave her a pacemaker. It was touch and go for a while, but she pulled through. I couldn't see going far away to school. I didn't want her to have to travel, and I didn't want to be so far away that I couldn't get to her quickly if I had to.

Right there, one of the toughest decisions of my basketball-playing career was made easy. I was staying home. I was going to Seton Hall University, which was less than fifteen minutes from home. Terry Dehere and Jerry Walker were there, which made it even easier for me.

But my mom's getting sick sealed it. I wasn't leaving her. I needed to play somewhere she could easily get to without getting on a plane or a bus. Seton Hall played their major games at what was then the Brendan Byrne Arena in the Meadowlands. Seton Hall U it was.

During the signing period right before basketball season started, we held a press conference and I announced that I was going to Seton Hall. The *Star-Ledger* and other local sportswriters were there. It was a big deal back then. But nothing like the way it is now with ESPN televising some of the early signings of big recruits. Our big deal included a couple of local reporters, my coach, and me.

My mother didn't really get all of the basketball stuff that was happening. She knew that it was an opportunity for me to maybe go pro. She also knew it was an opportunity for me to get an education, but she didn't know if my going to Seton Hall over Syracuse was a good move or not.

She liked that everybody knew who I was and that, as my mother, people knew her, too. She was a proud parent. My dad was, too. They used to come to my games—sitting in separate sections—and cheer me on. Sometimes we would even go out to eat together afterward. Basketball gave us back some of that "one big happy" feeling again . . . at least for a little while.

I was going to Seton Hall on a mission—to turn pro. I was going to work hard and become a millionaire, as I had seen so many before me do. I was going to give my mother a life she never imagined.

She'd tried to do everything in her power to make my life good. She'd tried to do right by me. So I wanted to do that for her. I guess it's every kid's dream to make it and be able to take care of and support his family. Most kids want to share that with their family. You have some kids who don't get along with their parents and can't wait to get out and don't care one way or the other what happens. But that wasn't me. No matter what went down, I wanted to do that for them. I guess it was a source of pride and would mean that I really made it.

I wanted my mother to not want for nothing. I wanted to be able to take care of her. I wanted to make sure that whatever she needed, I could get. I wanted to be the man.

8) DOWN THE HALL

You had to have a C average and at least a 700 on the SATs to get into college—any college. I had the C average but I didn't pass the SATs. I was a partial qualifier, which meant that I would be Prop 48 and would be ineligible to play basketball.

I guess I was lucky because had I graduated two years earlier, I would not even have had a scholarship. Originally, the NCAA instituted Prop 48 in 1986, they say, to increase graduation rates. Under the rule, if you didn't make the grade, not only would you not be allowed to practice or be a part of the team, but you would also be denied the scholarship. So if you wanted to play for that team, you would have to pay your own way that first year.

But a bunch of coaches, including John Thompson from Georgetown, protested and argued that the whole Prop 48 thing was biased and unfair because failing the standardized tests didn't necessarily mean that a student couldn't cut it academically on the college level. I always thought the SATs were racist anyway.

At least I got to keep my scholarship. I couldn't practice. I was just a student. It felt good, at first, to just be able to go to school. I know a lot of players who had to go to junior college or to some kind of prep school, but Seton Hall had enough faith in me to let me go there and get acclimated to their school and college life. They wanted me that bad that they would pay for me just to go to school. They cared about me as a student. At least, I think they cared. I appreciated it then and I definitely appreciate it now. The academic side is important.

Some believe that student athletes—especially football and basketball players on the Division I level— should be paid because when they win, they bring so much revenue to a school. I think education is pay enough. If you play well, you will get an opportunity to get paid. But if you go to college, then getting your degree or your education should be part of the plan. If you don't want to go to school, or if getting an education isn't important to you, then you can go and play overseas for a year or two and make money and prepare for the NBA. You don't have to go to college.

I was always against getting paid. I felt that they were giving me an education, and at a school such as Seton Hall, that equals $100,000 over four years, not to mention the gear, the food allowance, the room and board and books and everything else they cover in a scholarship. I had it good. And the time I put in there in the classroom, nobody can take that away from me. If an athlete is really smart, he should make sure to get his degree on that school's dime because basketball is not promised forever and at least you have something to fall back on.

I applaud the schools that allow their student athletes to go pro and still come back and get their degree later. Michael Jordan, Rasheed Wallace, and Vince Carter did that at North Carolina. Shaq went back, so did Michael Finley, and Damon Stoudamire.

Athletes really need to look at the big picture. You're getting an opportunity to play ball *and* get a college degree. A lot of athletes never think about what they will do after basketball. That's why so many of them are in the predicament they're in now—broke without options. They figure they're going to play ball forever. They aren't living in reality. What if you get hurt? What if you get sick? Do you have insurance on your knees? Do you have things set aside for the what-ifs?

I wish I had stayed and got my degree. Seton Hall didn't hold my scholarship after I left. When I went back, I had to pay out of my own pocket at a time when

I really didn't have it to pay. But I knew it was important. Thank God for a wealthy alumnus who helped me out and picked up the slack with my tuition and books.

I understand the game better today than I did when I was playing. I see that with an education these kids are putting themselves and their family in a position to really get rich. I hope those who leave early go back. I hope they learn from my mistakes because I definitely didn't see it that way when I was going to Seton Hall the first time.

At the time, it didn't matter or register with me. I was just happy to have a scholarship to eventually play basketball.

My first day on campus was my first taste of real college life. I had to take a few tests to figure out what my curriculum would be. We toured the campus and checked out the buildings and the dorms. At a freshman dance that night I got to meet other freshmen.

Those first few weeks were new and exciting and bittersweet.

In my mind, I was there to play basketball. Once the preseason started in October, I was depressed. What made it worse was that my roommate, Chris Davis, was on the team. He was from Virginia, and even though he was on the bench, he got to practice and to travel with the team. Chris kept me up to speed about how practice was going or what was happening and who was playing well and all of that. He was my good friend. He didn't rub it in, but it still hurt. For the first time in about seven years, basketball wasn't a part of my everyday life. I had either been playing in a summer league or on an AAU team or for my school.

I was still hanging with the players on the team now. They were my boys. But I started doing my own thing when they weren't around. I started drinking, partying, and cutting class.

Our team was a partying team, which made it easy for me. We created our own club in the dorms. Our dorm suite was a quad with two rooms and a common area between the two. Four of us shared a bathroom. We set up a bar in the common area, moved out all of the furniture, and had Club Xavier. We even had a dance floor. Thursday nights, when we weren't on the road, we were in Club Xavier. That was party night on campus.

We had people come from all over Jersey—from Essex County College, William Paterson, Fairleigh Dickinson. We only charged a dollar to get in. To this day, if you say Club Xavier, people will have a story and a memory.

And, yes, Lou Bee was on the one and twos. I was mixing my behind off. I put all of the energy I would have had for playing ball into keeping the party going. I spent more time partying and less time studying and going to class. I figured if I wasn't playing basketball, I was going to have some fun.

It all got back to Coach P. J. Carlesimo. He ended up taking it out on the team. When I cut class, the team had to run extra sprints and laps.

Chris pulled my coat and told me, "Yo, Lou Bee, even though you ain't here, we still have to break our asses for what you're not doing."

I felt bad. I had no idea. That woke me up. I realized that I had to stop doing what I was doing and get it together because there was still next year and my teammates didn't deserve to have to go through that because of me.

It got so bad that P.J. sent me to get "checked out." He wanted to know if something was wrong with me. It was the first time I had some sort of mental evaluation. They ran all of these diagnostic and psychological tests on me, and they all came back negative. I didn't get diagnosed until I got to the Jazz.

I had too much time on my hand and I started drinking and smoking weed a lot. P.J. had no idea how to talk to me or how to handle me. Sandy knew how to handle me. So did Coach Candelino from Elizabeth. He had a way of bringing me back to earth. If I cut class in high school, he would bench me. I cut class one time and that was it. I was so embarrassed having a hundred people asking me why I didn't play. I didn't want to go through that again, so I made it my business to make it to every class. Coach Candelino didn't yell and didn't curse at me, he simply benched me. I got the message.

P.J. didn't have a clue how to talk to me, and the more he yelled, the more I rebelled. But as the time approached for me to finally get to play, I buckled down and put the partying on pause. I knew what the consequences would be and I didn't want to lose another season.

That first year after sitting out was a struggle. When I got to Seton Hall, I was a trim 290 pounds. But not playing (and partying and eating all of the wrong things and smoking weed, which brought on the munchies), I put on fifty pounds in one year. Most have that Freshman Five. I had the Freshman Fifty.

That summer, P.J. pulled some strings and got me a tryout with USA Basketball. The World University Games were in London, England. I had never been outside the country before and I was excited to get to tour around jolly old England. Unfortunately, USA Basketball had our team on lock. They kept us separated from the country on a compound on some remote university campus. We couldn't leave. When we were allowed out, we had escorts, and everything—including the sightseeing—was controlled. We had lots of security with us every step of the way. But of course we managed to have fun among ourselves.

I was the youngest member on the team. My coach, P.J., was on the board of the Olympic committee and USA Basketball, so his intentions were to get me some playing time and exposure because I had to sit out that first year. He wanted me to get into shape and get me back my basketball feel. I was happy because it was a chance to travel and I knew I would get a chance to play.

The tryouts were in Mobile, Alabama, and all I remember is that it was hot. You could fry an egg on the concrete there. They drove us from Alabama to Louisiana to get our passports. All I was thinking was how country and how hot it was.

The tryouts were really not tryouts. The team was pretty much set. It was stacked with a bunch of All-Americans.

Roy Williams, the head coach of Kansas at the time, was the coach of Team USA. Bobby Hurley and Grant Hill from Duke, Alan Houston from Tennessee, Calbert Cheaney from Indiana, George Lynch and Hubert Davis from North Carolina, and Adonis Jordan from the University of Kansas were on the team with me.

We had so much fun blowing out every team we played. I put up some good numbers, averaging eight points, six rebounds, and two blocks. Not bad considering I hadn't much played in a year. We played Canada in the finals and I think we won by forty points. Our average margin of victory was thirty-five.

By the time I came back for the season, I was in much better shape. But P.J. never stopped riding me. I guess he was disappointed, which he had every right to be. It didn't start clicking for me until the Big East Tournament of that year. That's when the whole team started gelling.

It wasn't as if we were losing a whole lot beforehand. We just weren't playing well together, and P.J.'s coaching style was taking all of the fun out of basketball for me. I was used to being the center of the offense. Every team I had played on up until this point—except for St. Anthony—the plays ran through me. I was the first option. I was the one they looked to for most of the scoring. On this team, P.J. used me like a role player. He kept me on the bench a lot and put me in for garbage time. Yes, we had some good players on the team, but I wasn't a slouch.

P.J. was such a perfectionist. If you missed an assignment or made a mental mistake, you came out of the game and sat for a while. I wasn't used to being on the bench so much, either.

I was actually thinking about transferring. But he came through with a big blessing for me—an invitation from USA Basketball to represent my country in the Junior Olympics.

This was the year of the Dream Team, featuring Michael Jordan, Larry Bird, Magic Johnson, David Robinson. It was an NBA All-Star team, and the world got to see who was really the best. I think the other countries got cocky because they were beating our college players the previous two Olympics. So when we came in with the Dream Team, it was a wrap. Blow-out city. Gold medal. P.J. and Coach K., Krzyzewski, from Duke University, were assistant coaches on the Dream Team.

I got invited to play in Spain on the Junior Olympics team and was excited.

The tryouts were held in New Jersey at Upsala College (which was in East Orange and has since closed). They put us up in the Hilton at Short Hills across from the mall. It was funny because this was my stomping ground, yet we were restricted and couldn't go where we wanted. We had an escort to go to the mall. It was crazy. They were about their business to make sure we wouldn't get distracted.

It worked. We followed the lead of the Dream Team and blew out our opponents in every game, winning the championship.

The USA wasn't well liked back then on the international level in basketball. All the teams came out gunning for us—not that they had a chance. Our toughest game was against Spain, and we beat them by five points. They had a bunch of pros playing on their team. But we were able to turn it up and came away with the victory for another gold medal.

I learned a lot from that experience.

I felt proud standing on the podium while they played our national anthem getting that gold medal around my neck. It was the first time in my life that I felt really connected to my country. You feel connected to your family and to your hood, but being in this foreign country where people weren't really feeling us, and playing hard and winning and having our flag raised and hearing the national anthem, it all had meaning. They play the national anthem all the time at basketball games in the States, but nothing's like hearing it among a crowd of people who aren't connected to it. It's just you and your teammates and that flag. I was an American that day first—a gold medalist representing my country.

I was riding high coming from that experience and ran right into a brick wall—P. J. Carlesimo. I had so much fun with Team USA and the guys—many of whom I still keep in touch with. After such a special bond and with my love for basketball at an all-time high, coming back to Seton Hall to play was a downer in some ways.

I came back feeling that I was great, and P.J. would remind me every day that I had a lot of work to do. I don't want to kick dirt on P.J., but he would say things about me in the paper, like I could have rebounded more in this game or played better defense or something, that added to my feelings of wanting to leave. He used this tactic to try to tweak me to make me play better. I think a lot of coaches do that. They try to light a fire to get their players to do more. They try to make them mad enough to go out and prove them wrong. That just wasn't a good tactic for me. It made me want to do the opposite. I wouldn't say anything. I couldn't. P.J. was my coach and I had to respect him. But I didn't like playing for him. It was extrafrustrating.

He couldn't get away with that today. Not with the way these players are. As a matter of fact, I believe that P.J. didn't get away with his style much when he coached on the pro level. While P.J. was the coach of the Golden State Warriors, didn't Latrell Sprewell choke him for saying something Latrell didn't like?

While I played for P.J., I just swallowed it. All the things that players do today, publicly criticizing their coach, I was taught to never do that. So while he trashed me, I said nothing.

It was a tough adjustment. He was a tough coach. P.J. was very different from Coach Candelino. At Elizabeth, while I was certainly still developing and had a lot to learn, my coach was much more gentle in letting me know what to do. Not P.J.

I respect the man, though. I was with him for three years. He was a good coach. He knew the game. He was a professional on and off the court. He cared about us. P.J. made us team-minded. He taught us to watch each other's back. He promoted a team atmosphere. At Seton Hall we did everything together. We played together, we ate together, we even hung out together—even the white guys on the team. We partied as hard with the white guys as we did with the blacks. It felt like a team—as if all my teammates were my brothers. My white teammates used to come to our Thursday-night parties at Club Xavier. I have some good memories. I went to my first Broadway play with Jim Dickinson and Daryl Crist, two of my white teammates. We went to see *Miss Saigon*.

I had a lot of firsts at Seton Hall. I went to my first toga party at Seton Hall. I learned how to swim at Seton Hall.

And I had my first hit of cocaine on campus. I didn't get hooked on the stuff then, but that was definitely the beginning.

In my sophomore year of play, my third at the

school, we won the Big East Championship. But there were stories and whispers that I wasn't living up to my hype. Seton Hall was supposed to win a bunch of national titles with me on the team. But we didn't make it far my first year, and by my junior year, while we won our second straight Big East title, we were bounced in the Sweet Sixteen. We were favored that year to go at least to the Final Four and we were upset by Western Kentucky.

P.J. blamed me. The dude I was guarding was quicker than me, and P.J. kept playing us in a man-to-man defense instead of going to the zone. My guy was scoring, taking me to the basket, and I ended up in foul trouble. So I was on the bench while Western Kentucky was beating us. Western Kentucky ended up losing to Florida State in the next round.

North Carolina won it all that year, beating Michigan's Fab Five in the finals. Most will remember that game because those five freshmen from Michigan almost did their thing. Most will remember the time-out Chris Webber called that Michigan didn't have. But they played a helluva game. We were supposed to be there.

That was the best finish Western Kentucky probably ever had. They really haven't won anything since. In fact, Seton Hall really hasn't done anything since I left, either.

After the game, I declared myself eligible for the draft.

I felt that I could play in the NBA. I didn't want

to listen to P.J., or anyone else, anymore. I knew what I needed to do. That was my mentality. People were telling me I should stay. Win a championship. I would get more money in the draft and be a higher pick if I waited. I was hardheaded. If I coulda, woulda, shoulda, I would have stayed. That would have been a smarter decision. We would probably have won a championship and I would probably have been a No. 1 pick. But I wasn't thinking long-term.

I wanted it all now.

9) MORE MONEY, MORE PROBLEMS

When I declared I was turning pro, my high school coach, Ben Candelino, connected with an agent friend of his, Sal DiFazio. He said Sal knew the ropes and that he would be a good choice for me. Sal was a Jersey guy, a family man. He seemed like a good guy. He had represented other big men, such as Charles Shackleford and Jayson Williams. So I gave him a shot.

Sal told me that I would probably be a first-round lottery pick and definitely a first-round overall pick. He told me that I would be getting millions and that he would take care of me. I believed him. I signed with him right before I got drafted, and he went to work. Sal set up the workouts with the Nets, Charlotte Hornets, and Atlanta Hawks.

A lot of guys were getting in trouble for getting money from agents while they were still in school and all of that. I never got any money directly from Sal until after I signed with Utah.

That day was a blur. It was me and Sal and Larry Miller, the owner of the Jazz. I got to meet Coach Jerry Sloan for the first time that day, too. Everyone was nice.

I remember there being several copies of my contracts in the room, and I was supposed to sign all of them on the dotted line. I didn't have any concept of what I was signing. I didn't read it. Sal told me the terms. But even that was a blur. All I heard was $5 million.

A millionaire. A multimillionaire at the stroke of a pen.

I signed on the dotted line of my contract to play basketball for the Utah Jazz and knew I was officially a millionaire. I was beaming and thinking in that moment about what I was going to buy. The money is not supposed to come immediately, but it did. I was able to go shopping immediately. Sal handed me a wad of cash and I went to the mall and tried to buy something but couldn't find anything I really wanted. I just wanted to buy something. I wanted to feel that freedom to just go in the store and not have to worry about what something cost.

Most star athletes already knew that feeling. Most of them had "bank" before even turning pro.

You're not supposed to have an agent, but many of the star athletes "signed" with agents before turning pro, and those agents made sure the athlete was well taken care of. I have known some players who have got $100,000 from their agent way before they declared that they were turning pro.

All they would have to say is "I want to buy a car," and the agent would make sure they got that car. The agent would hide the connection by putting the car in someone else's name.

That's how that worked. The agent gave you money or whatever you wanted but was betting on your making millions in the NBA and charging you interest on the money and the things you got.

You're a kid, so you don't think about such things as "interest," and that it's just a loan.

As soon as I signed on the dotted line, the floodgates opened.

"Sal, I need a nice ride," I told him.

The next day, I was in a 1993 Land Cruiser. I put a fly system in it.

"Sal, I want this place," and I was moving in. Everything was taken care of. I picked out furniture, it was delivered.

After a few months I was homesick, so I decided to move home out to Utah. I brought my whole family out there to live with me. They couldn't fit in my apartment, so I said, "Ma, go pick out your house."

She found one of the biggest houses in the South

Jordan neighborhood of Salt Lake City. It was in a developing community where people were building their homes from scratch, and she had few neighbors. It was the biggest house I had ever seen. Our next-door neighbor on the right had horses. The neighbor on the other side had a basketball court and a tennis court, and he was one of the heads of the Mormon Church. Another neighbor down the road had three wives and twenty kids. But these houses were spread out.

Of course, we were the only blacks there. It was country. It had a lot of land, acres and acres. I didn't know what an acre was then.

The house was beautiful, yellow and brown, with a three-car garage with a huge driveway. It had an Olympic-size, heated pool with a Jacuzzi and trampoline and basketball court in the back. I had two kennels built for my dog.

My mother and stepfather had a suite with a dual shower. I took the basement and tricked it out into a mini-apartment. My sister had her own room. My brother had his own room that had a deck.

When my mother picked out this house, I went to Sal and said, "This is the house my mother wants." And we got it. I don't remember signing a bunch of paperwork or going through the hassles of credit checks and title searches and all of that. A few weeks later, we had the keys and were moving in.

We were like George and Weezy and Lionel. We had moved on up.

I didn't experience the boosters and the agents and all of that kind of cash that some highly recruited players across the country were getting. I didn't get a car like LeBron or a house for my moms. I stayed away from all of that. I got through Seton Hall without any scandals or problems. I took pride in staying out of trouble in that area. Outside of cocaine, I tried to keep my nose clean.

So turning pro was my coming-out party. I moved from lettuce to fries.

When you're in the pros, whatever you need is taken care of. You pick up the phone and say, "My name is Luther Wright . . . ," and it just happens. And this was before computers and all of the technology we have now. I would have had crazy stuff if technology were available. No one ever told me no. Whatever I asked for, I got.

And they have the nerve to give you meal money on top of the millions. You would get your meal money according to how much you signed for or where you were drafted. We would get it every two weeks. I would get $1,800 every two weeks. Some players got more.

Then there was all of the free stuff—the free sneakers, gear, sweat suits, socks. We got special treatment when we went out to restaurants and clubs. Some places would feel that "Hey, you got money, pay your way." But most of the time, we were treated like VIPs—free drinks and the whole nine. That was the best part of being in the NBA. The other part was doing things for my friends and family.

It wasn't enough to buy things for me. Once I got my mother a house, she needed something to get around in. I bought her a 1993 Mercury Marquis. Of course, we went clothes shopping. I gave my family cash to buy whatever they wanted. My mother bought herself a mink. You know it's cold in Utah.

Everyone was just chilling. Just living. Whatever my friends and family needed, they got it. I didn't put them on an allowance. I just called Sal, and in a day or that day I was handed an envelope with cash.

The freedom to be able to buy whatever I wanted was like a drug.

Looking back, I should have paid closer attention. At the least, I should have cared. I was extremely lucky that Sal DiFazio was the kind of man that he was. So many athletes get taken to the hoop with their finances. The statistics show that something like 70 percent of NBA players are broke just three years after they leave the league. That's crazy.

But I understand how it happens. You're young. You come from the hood, where you're not used to having this kind of money. Nobody in your family understands real finances or what to do with the money. You want the things you see everybody in the league with, and you want it now. And you have an agent, who doesn't tell you the truth.

The truth: Any money they "give" you comes with a heavy price and heavy interest. That money they "gave" you before you turned pro, they will collect on, too—with interest. They will take their percentage out of each contract. By the time you finish buying the things you want, you're broke. You can't ever get back full value for cars and jewelry. The things you do to your home to trick it out don't usually pay back, either—especially in a depressed housing market. Where can you get back the millions on a home like that? Who's buying it?

The athletes don't read the contract. They don't do their homework. I didn't know that an agent was only supposed to get 3 or 4 percent, and not 10 percent, which I was giving Sal, or the 15 percent some other players were paying their agents.

Your mother is there, but she just wants you to get that money so everyone can enjoy the fruits. She's not reading the fine print, either. And what background does she have in finance?

We athletes get blindsided by the number. The amount. We think that money will last forever. Some agents are so slick. They won't take their cut from the first contract. They will let it collect even more interest.

But Sal, I must say, did me a solid. He did many things from a human standpoint. He went beyond what a typical agent would do.

Nearly twenty years after leaving the NBA, I'm still living off that money. I definitely appreciate Mr. Di-Fazio. I have nothing bad to say about him.

I could easily have been one of those statistics if not for him. To have a man make sure that I was taken care

of for the long haul is just great. He spread those payments out for twenty-five years so no matter what, I
would have something.

I would have smoked it all up in less than a year if
not for Sal. My family would definitely have spent it up
if I didn't (and don't think they didn't try). Instead, I get
a check every month, like an annuity.

Sal was my agent, my broker, my bank teller. My
friend.

Unfortunately, after I left Utah, my mother stepped
in and took power of attorney over my affairs. She had
control over all of my money and made a mess of it,
as if she had graduated from Howard, Harvard, or the
Wharton School of business. (I love you, Ma! But you
know . . .) All the things Sal put into place for me, she
single-handedly undid.

She somehow managed to borrow against the lump
sum that I would be drawing on for twenty-five years,
decreasing my monthly payments from around $15,000
a month to just over a $1,000 a month. I went from liv-
ing comfortably for the rest of my life to seeing it all
fade away.

Of course, I played a major role in all of that. Because
it wasn't just the breakdown mentally, it was the drug
abuse. I came back to New Jersey broken and decided to
check out. I went on a drug binge that lasted years.

I made a willful and conscious decision to not give a
fuck anymore. I decided that basketball didn't matter. I
was shortsighted.

It started almost as soon as I got to Utah. I often wondered if I had been drafted by Jersey or another team, where would I be? But this was the hand I was dealt, and now I'm grateful to have an opportunity few people ever get—to start over. God put me there for a reason. Now I have this story to tell.

10) ROOKIE BLUES

Right after the draft and the partying in Detroit, I flew home with my peeps, packed my stuff, and was off to Utah. Sal went with me on this first trip. I had to be at rookie camp and get settled. NBA rookie camp is normally in a different city each year. I guess they like to spread around that NBA wealth. This year, it was in Salt Lake City, Utah, which should have made my transition a whole lot easier.

The first week of rookie camp, the NBA held seminars where they tried to prepare us for what was to come. In a classroom setting they had different speakers, mostly former NBA players, come in to talk to us about everything from traveling to groupies. They even talked to us about watching out for certain people who might try to take advantage of us or be our friend or in our camp because they saw the money. I was there, I was hearing it, but I wasn't really listening. I thought I could handle it all and that I didn't need their "lessons" on what to watch out for.

The first few weeks of being a rookie were a blur. Everything was happening so quickly—I was drafted, I signed, I was in a new city, I was in rookie camp. I didn't really have time to process it all.

Sal left a day after we got there, and I had to learn a lot on my own. While the NBA had these seminars, I didn't have anyone close to me to hold my hand through them. I was learning as I went along. I was nervous and excited, but in my mind this wasn't it. This wasn't the big league, yet. I knew that. But it was close enough.

I was soaking it all in, trying to learn as much as I could. It was a competitive summer league. People showed up, packing the arena to see us play. We had one of the most popular summer leagues. We were playing against other teams in the league, and we came close to winning that summer-league tournament. There was no prize. But there was recognition.

At night, there were the parties. I always found out where the hot spots were. My first week there, I went to a corner liquor store and said to someone standing around outside, "Yo, where the weed at?"

When you're from the hood, you always know where to go and whom to ask. I wasn't going to ask any of my teammates because I didn't know them like that then. And I wasn't asking a Mormon priest. I knew where to go and I got my answer.

I was hooked up with my drug connection from day one. That wasn't good because I was smoking just about every day. I thought I was slick. I thought I was doing a good job of hiding it until things started to unravel. As I think back, a lot of the bad decisions I made could definitely have had to do with my smoking too much weed.

But I was in such a haze—both from the weed and the huge shift in my life from moving to Utah—that I wasn't seeing things clearly.

I enjoyed rookie camp. I got to play. I thought I was doing my thing. Initially, I was adjusting well. I found a place in downtown Salt Lake City on the twenty-third floor in a condominium overlooking the city. A penthouse, it had great views. It was two bedrooms, two bathrooms. I shared my bachelor's pad with my stepbrother until I decided to move the rest of my family to Utah.

This was definitely different from the dorms at Seton Hall or the hotels I was used to staying in. This was my first place. I owned this. I told Sal this was where I wanted to live, and that week I had the keys and a deed.

This place had a Jacuzzi on the roof. I didn't spend much time in it, but it was nice having it. It was nice flossing. It was nice saying it was mine.

But that feeling of being on top of the world and having it all left me once the real season started. Once I got with the whole team and the Utah Jazz system, I went from top of the world to end of the bench.

11) AND ALL THAT JAZZ

stayed in Utah after rookie camp. I had my new
bachelor's pad and my stepbrother, Ricky, was with
me. We hung out until veterans' camp started. That's
when the whole team would be there.

The week before that, after the NBA rookie tournament ended, Utah's rookies stayed in state and worked
out. We learned plays and prepared for the veterans'
arrival. We were back doing two-a-days. When the vets
arrived, we practiced with them for a week. The atmosphere changed immediately. It went from semirelaxed
to all-business. I guess Utah was really serious about
winning a championship, and the older players didn't
want any fun and games. It got corny for me quickly.

I also came into camp with a cloud over my head.

After playing well in rookie camp, the week before the vets showed up I started experiencing shortness of breath and heart palpitations. Maybe it was the high altitude or maybe it was the intensity of the two-a-days. I got checked out and the doctors told me to rest.

The team flew to Hawaii for preseason camp. I stayed behind for a couple of days before rejoining. I was anxious to get to Hawaii. I wanted to be in the mix. But I had also never been to Hawaii before. It was as beautiful as any posters I had ever seen of the place. It was just like what you see in the movies.

You get off the airplane, and they put the lei around your neck and you want to experience everything—the luau, the black-sand beaches, and everything you ever heard about Hawaii. I went scuba diving. I even went surfing. I wanted to try because it looked like fun. I had never done it before, so I went to the beach, rented a surfboard, and they gave me a few instructions. Then I surfed some teeny-weeny waves.

Even basketball was fun in Hawaii. We played against the Lakers and I got to meet James Worthy, Vlade Divac, Byron Scott, and A. C. Green. We beat them a couple of times. I felt that I was really in the big leagues. I finally got to play with everyone and I played well.

I thought, *I can really play in this league.* I was looking forward to getting the season started. As long as I was playing, in shape, producing, winning (I loved winning), and hanging with my teammates, it was great. I enjoyed that.

I loved winning. I won two gold medals—one in the Junior Olympics and one at the World University Games. I don't have a single medal or any of that memorabilia anymore. But I know I did it. I experienced it. I will tell my grandkids about it. I can look back now and appreciate all that I accomplished.

I loved winning, but I didn't necessarily love the work that it took sometimes to be a winner.

Around the time we came back to Utah, I got into the daily grind of preseason and the routine of everything. I wasn't making a lot of friends on my team, my coaches weren't feeling me, and I wasn't getting a chance to play. It stopped being fun. It went from fun and games to a job.

Before this I looked at basketball as a hobby that paid me. I could wake up and shoot a jump hook. I could rebound and dunk in my sleep. Now I had to prepare plays, study tapes, memorize game plans. And with all of that there was no guarantee that I would get to play. I had to work for it. I felt that I couldn't do it. This was real work.

Besides working with my father on the streets of Jersey City, I never really held a job before in my life—not a real nine-to-five type of job where I had to be accountable. I had coaches in the past that understood me or, if they didn't, would hand me off to others who did. As long as I played, we were cool. But it was a different game on the pro level.

Or maybe it was just different with the Utah Jazz. I

wouldn't know because I never had the opportunity to play for another pro team. Part of my problem was Utah itself. The culture shock. I was away from my comfort zone, my peoples, my neighborhood, thrown into this lily-white environment with few familiar outlets.

I remember going to the mall during my first days in Utah and thinking, *Where are all the black people?* I mean, I was the only one in the mall that day who was black, and it was weird and scary. Imagine coming from basically an all-black or very multicultural environment into that. And having people stare at you because you're seven feet two inches.

Playing ball also probably stopped being fun for me because I wasn't mature. I needed to grow up. I didn't want to. I was now a professional basketball player. I didn't much care for the professional part; I just wanted to play. I was a big kid. (Still am, in many ways.)

It was depressing for me in Utah. It was almost like prison. We had to get up at six thirty in the morning. We would grab breakfast between seven and seven thirty, then have our first meetings around eight.

I was leaving the house to go to work, and some mornings it was still dark out. My parents, my brothers, and my sister would still be in bed, all comfy and cozy, sleeping, kicking back, chilling, without a care in the world. They had no place to go and nothing to do but enjoy life. They were reaping the benefits of my hard work and doing nothing to preserve it.

While they were enjoying life, I was out there

working hard, getting yelled at, in the gym for two hours of grueling practice and then meetings and then working out and training some more. Then I had a few hours to rest and eat, then we were back in the gym for two-plus more hours of practice. This was preseason training camp, which came after I had already gone through rookie camp.

I was on a team of veterans and everyone was serious. They were a player or two away from being a championship team, and I was initially looked at as one of those missing pieces. A lot of expectations were on me and I wasn't ready, willing, or able to meet those expectations.

I had gone through a whirlwind summer. I was drafted in June and I was doing a lot of media (and partying). I had to go to Utah and find a place to live. I had to think about what to do with my family. Then I had rookie camp, which was a shock to my system. I had never worked that hard in my life.

By the time I made it to Hawaii with the rest of my team, I was met with a newspaper article in which Karl Malone had said some stuff about me. Malone gave an interview to a local newspaper and they asked him about me, and Malone said something like "They paid him all of this money and he's not showing up? He's starting off on the wrong foot."

I had never met Karl Malone. I had never even spoken to him. He didn't know me and I know he couldn't possibly know why I wasn't in camp. That left a bad taste in my mouth. He didn't know what was going on with me, but felt that he could say something about me.

By the time I made it to camp, I was on the defensive.

So that first day in camp—after I finished playing, surfing, and going to luaus—was tense for me. I walked into the gym and I started thinking, *Oh, boy, where am I at?* There were John Stockton, Tyrone Corbin, Tom Chambers. And there was Karl Malone. And there was me—the new guy.

I had a lot of pressure to live up to. They were looking at me as if I were supposed to be some sort of savior.

To his credit, Karl Malone came to me and tried to make me feel welcome. He didn't apologize for what he said about me in the paper, but he did tell me how it went down. He said they stuck a mic in his face and he was caught off guard. What he wanted to tell me was "Come on, big fella. Come on to camp so we can beat you up and get you into shape."

We were cool after that.

But Coach Jerry Sloan and I weren't cool. I discovered that first practice that he was a yeller. *Oh, boy!* I wasn't good with people yelling at me. It would make me rebel in a quiet (and eventually a not-so-quiet) way. I started cutting off my nose to spite my face. The more Coach Sloan yelled, the less motivated I became. I would come up with phantom injuries and ailments and excuses for why I missed an assignment or why I missed practice. Every time I missed practice, it would cost me playing time. It got to the point where I wasn't playing at all that first season. When I did play, I didn't play well. I ended up averaging less than two points a game.

Instead of sucking it up and working harder, I became rebellious. I guess I thought in my mind at the time that I would show them. I wasn't giving my all. I was lackluster. I turned to drugs. I was smoking weed every day.

One day, I missed practice because I had a legitimate dental appointment. I had an impacted wisdom tooth and had it taken care of, but I forgot to tell the team officials. I was home recuperating, chilling and smoking (which I wasn't supposed to do after dental work), and my doorbell rang.

It was Coach Sloan and Coach Scott Layden. They came to check up on me. I didn't have time to air out my place, so I had to let them in. It must have smelled like a weed factory. I tried to play it off and they didn't say anything, but I know they smelled it. They left and the next day I got hit with a fine for missing practice.

They seemed to be less tolerant after that surprise visit. I thought the fine was a bunch of BS. I had a legitimate excuse, but I think they were trying to send me a message to get my act together. But it had the opposite effect.

I wasn't thinking. I felt that I had all of this money, and I could do what I wanted. I was dealing with a bunch of females at the time. I was a pretty popular dude. I was rich and doing what I pleased. What could they do to me?

As my first NBA season was under way, instead of being that missing piece on a championship team, I found myself on the bench and in the doghouse.

It felt like my freshman year at Seton Hall when I was Prop 48. I was part of the team, but not really. I wasn't included or involved, so I checked out. I continued smoking and partying and started hanging out with the wrong crowd.

Leave it to me to find drug dealers to make friends with in Utah. I figured that I was going to bring some of Jersey to Utah, and I was going to find Jersey in Utah. I started hanging out with pimps, gangbangers, and hooligans. I was partying and getting high every day. I was doing everything but what I was there to do—play basketball.

Instead of hanging out with the veterans on my team and learning from them, I preferred the company of these other people.

My teammates tried to talk to me. Bryon Russell, who was my boy, tried hard. We were in rookie camp together and I liked him. But I was hardheaded. I wasn't listening to anyone. Everything he said about my throwing away this opportunity and having a chance to do something that people only dream about went in one ear and out the other.

I would go hang with my pimp and gang friends and go to the club and take over the deejay booth or go find whatever girl I was with that week and spend the night with her. My mind wasn't on basketball.

Sal was somewhat taking my side and making it easier for me to justify what I was doing.

"I wish we were in a different situation," he would say, instead of telling me to make the best of it and make it work. He didn't like Utah for me. I didn't like Utah for me.

Eventually, Utah didn't like Utah for me.

12) OUT OF BOUNDS

When you start to spiral out of control, you don't usually recognize it while you're in midspiral. I was so delusional about what was going on with me that I made one bad decision after another. But at least I was consistent. I was doing it in every area of my life—my career and my personal.

While I was fouling out in basketball, I thought I was doing my thing with the ladies. Looking back, I was just as foul in that area, too. Juggling everything else I was trying to juggle and adjust in my life and adding women to the mix made it even harder.

I never saw myself getting married. I never understood what it meant to be a husband, or even a good boyfriend. I didn't know how to treat women. I wasn't physically abusive or anything like that. I was just never there and not really connected to the women I was with. Just as I wanted to do what I wanted to do on the courts, I carried that same attitude into my relationships. I didn't want anyone checking me or telling me what to do. If a woman got in the way of that, I was gone. I was on my own time, in my own space. I would say things to women because I just didn't care. To say I wasn't a gentleman is an overstatement.

I was never a suave dude, smooth with the ladies. But I did all right. I always had a girlfriend, or two or three. But I was far from a player, especially compared to some of my boys in the NBA.

A lot of my teammates and friends in the NBA had their pick of the groupie litter. There was plenty to pick from.

It would not be unusual to show up at a hotel and have ladies waiting in the lobby, in the bar and restaurant, even in the hallways of our room floors.

I didn't have any groupies at Seton Hall. There weren't girlies waiting around the locker room or the dorms. We had our fans, but nothing like what I saw when I got to the NBA.

We had one away game in Oakland against the Golden State Warriors my first week in the league. When we came to the hotel, a bunch of women were in the lobby. They had an *Ebony* fashion show at the hotel, too, so I didn't think anything of it. But then I noticed a difference in the women. You could clearly tell who was a professional model, there for the fashion show, and who was there for us.

Most of the women were there for us.

They were just hanging out. I went upstairs and came back down to get something to eat and the *Ebony* women weren't there anymore. The other women were just sitting there waiting, watching. It was a barlike atmosphere. They were looking. I was looking. I didn't approach anyone. I knew they were there for something. No party was going on. It wasn't my kind of scene. It seemed kind of desperate. I wasn't comfortable around women who were so out there like that and aggressive. So I went back up to my room.

In other cities, it was the same thing. By the third city, I got used to it. I started to strike up a conversation with a few of the women. But my teammates made me aware of the situation. "Be careful. We're going to this town and the groupies will be out. They travel in packs and they just show up," one of them told me.

They were right. Every city, more women!

The Bullets (now the Wizards) in D.C. had the best groupies, and of course La-La Land, Los Angeles. New York and Atlanta had theirs, too, of course. But D.C. and L.A. stood out. The ladies there were all fly, and all tens in just about every market we went to. But in D.C. and L.A. they had a certain air. They were more sophisticated and seemed to know exactly what they wanted.

I wasn't into the groupie lifestyle. I was into having

one lady in a town. I liked knowing when I got to that town that I would have someone who knew me, whom I could relax with, party with, and have some fun with. I might have met someone at a club or a function or a party, and I would hold on to her. When I came to town, that would be my lady that I hung out with.

After the draft, I met a lady at that party that Chris Webber threw in Detroit. Then I was off to rookie orientation, which was in Orlando. I met someone there, too, in a club. So now I had a friend in Detroit and Orlando.

They warned us about the groupies during rookie orientation, which was a conference-type setting where a bunch of different speakers talked to us about the ins and outs of NBA life. Some of them spoke about their experiences with drugs and alcohol. I listened, but I wasn't paying attention to all of that. My mind was on other things—such as the next party I was going to or the next woman I would meet.

They were telling us to watch for the pimps, too, because they said that they would want to be our friends. It was informative. But I guess I wasn't trying to hear that because I ended up hanging out with the pimps. I was young and I wanted to hang out where the party was. The pimps always knew where the parties were.

And the women? They just came along with everything else. I wasn't serious with any of them. I definitely was never in love—although I'm sure some of them thought I was. I might have said it to a few once or twice. But I did a couple of women very wrong (and a few got me back tenfold).

I had a girlfriend who lived in Philadelphia. She was my main lady. I moved her out to Utah with me, and when I moved back to Jersey, I stayed with her. We met at a Greek picnic in south Jersey and just hit it off. She was beautiful, had long hair and a laid-back personality.

She got pregnant while we were living together in Philly. I was excited about having a baby until the baby actually came. We had a little girl. She was beautiful and I loved her, but the whole fatherhood, husband, responsibility thing was getting to be too much.

I promised to marry her. I told her we were engaged, but I never broke down and got the ring. She had settled into this routine with me.

Pam (not her real name) worked at a print shop where she did silk screens. I used to drop off the baby at day care, then drop Pam off at work, so I could have the car for the day until it was time to pick up Pam and the baby. This went on for about eight months. One day, we dropped the baby off at day care; I then dropped off Pam at work. I hopped on I-95 North and never looked back.

I never called, I never wrote, I never saw her after that.

She called like crazy, but I didn't return her calls.

Why did I walk out on her and my baby like that? It's the place where I was at the time is all I can give as an explanation. I was foul. I was smoking a lot of weed and just didn't care about anyone but myself.

I have no excuse. I had a drug problem; I could blame it on that. But I think more was going on.

Pam was on me all of the time about smoking weed. She was right. But again, being hardheaded, I didn't want to hear from anybody telling me anything.

"Why are you tripping?" I would constantly tell her. "I got this."

But she wouldn't stop. She cared about me and wanted to make sure I was taking care of myself so I could be there for our daughter. I think the night before I left we had an argument over my weed smoking. Actually, she lectured me because I had tuned her out completely and didn't say much of anything. I just kept smoking my weed.

When I left, she hadn't seen it coming. I mean, who just up and leaves like that?

I didn't handle pressure and tension well. I didn't have any order. I was out of order. I was feeling pretty powerless after losing my life in Utah. Maybe doing this gave me a sense of power. I was being defiant and doing exactly what I wanted to do, being my own man.

When I got back to Jersey, I met another girlie. I started living with her in Newark. I had officially moved back home with my mother, but that was getting tired. I used women at this time to escape—escape from my mother's nagging, escape from having to face myself.

The woman I moved in with in Newark was into going to church. I would go to church with her from time to time. One Sunday, I didn't want to go. She left me in the house.

When I moved in with her, I had my stuff packed in big green garbage bags. I took those same garbage bags and packed my clothes. I locked her door, left her a note: *I can't do this no more. I'm going back home.* I walked to my mom's house. The woman called me. She talked me into coming back. I moved back in with her for a couple of weeks, then left her for good.

I even got married during this period . . . for a month. I had no concept of marriage and it was all a big game for me. I knew Sheila (not her real name) wanted to get married, and I wanted to stay with her, so I gave her what she wanted. But it wasn't what I wanted and the whole marriage thing wasn't real to me.

This woman used to sing in the Samaritans, a gospel group that I had been in on and off since high school. I started talking to this girl while we were in the group together. When I came home from Utah, we reconnected when I started singing with the group again. I used to drive her home after rehearsals. I told my mother that I thought I wanted to marry her. She was a nice girl. So I figured, why not marry her?

I went to Irvington to one of the fake-gold jewelry stores in the Irvington Center and bought her a fake-diamond engagement ring. She bought the wedding bands—his and her wedding rings.

She wasn't a bad girl. But I never treated her right. I don't even remember proposing to her. I was probably high. We got married three months after we started going together.

The day before we got married, we were in my mother's Cadillac in Livingston and ended up on JFK Boulevard near the Short Hills Mall. My mother got pulled over. Her car wasn't registered and didn't have any insurance. I hadn't taken care of my business the way I should have. I bought people nice things, but didn't cross my T's and dot my I's.

My mother got locked up. My future wife came and bailed her out. I appreciated her being there for us like that and wanted to make the relationship work.

We got married the following week. Looking back, I think the drugs again played a major part. I had graduated from smoking weed to smoking cocaine regularly by this time and was probably high most of the time. We got married in a church in north Newark. My uncle took a video of it (I think he still has the VHS). But it was so fake. I think I was high during the whole ceremony and definitely afterward.

I hid my drug use from her. She had no clue that I got high. Her father was a minister and he married us. It lasted less than a month.

Let me tell you what happened in those thirty days. I had this nice big house on Webster Street in Irvington. She was living on Broadway in Newark over a paint store. She lived there with her parents and her sister. Her mother and father were in one room. She and her sister shared the other. I told her to come move in with me on Webster Street.

It was great for those thirty days. She cleaned, she cooked—she made me cheesecake and fried chicken. I was loving that part of married life. But my house was hectic. Not only was my new wife staying with me, but also my mother, my sister, my sister's husband, and their kids. There was a lot of noise and then the arguments started. I wasn't paying enough attention to her, I wasn't helping her around the house, I wasn't doing this and I wasn't doing that. I hated all of that jabbering, so I would say something rude and she would run back to her parents' place crying. I refused to drive her, so she'd have to take two buses to get to her parents.

Her father called me the last time we had a fight and told me, "We're going to disappear and you won't see her anymore if you keep this up."

He felt that I was abusing his little girl and I was. I was mentally abusing her. I treated her like my maid, not my wife. I was making her wash the clothes, clean the house, cook for me, wash my feet, and even wait on my mother hand and foot. She wasn't feeling that. She would call her mother.

This one time, after she came back from her runaway to her parents, I had just come back from powdering my nose. When I came in the door, she was coming up the stairs. She said something like "Where you been?" I said I was out with my boys. She started getting in my face. I grabbed at her and she fell down the stairs.

She got up, left, and I haven't seen her since. That was in 1997. I never tried to get in touch with her and I never filed for a formal divorce. Come to find out, I was so high, I never filed the proper papers to be married in the first place. So I was never legally married.

While I was doing my dirt, I was building up some bad karma. It all came back to me. All of the bad I put out, I definitely got back. I have nothing to say except . . . I'm sorry!

13) BLOCKED SHOT

The headlines called it a nervous breakdown. The papers had a field day with reports of my being in the middle of nowhere naked and out of control. The stories brought up the hope and promise I came with to Utah and how I was probably the biggest disappointment the team had ever had. I wasn't just a dud, I was a pariah. I was an embarrassment.

Well, the news reports got the story half-right. What really hurt was that no one ever bothered to ask, Why? Why did I do all of those crazy things? It was too easy to write me off as being crazy. But that wasn't it.

For months leading up to my "nervous breakdown," I had been depressed. Utah can do that to a person. It wasn't Utah the state—because I can honestly say that the people were nice to me and Salt Lake City welcomed me with open arms. But playing for the Jazz and Jerry Sloan was too much for me to handle. So I did what I always did when I found myself in a difficult situation—I looked for an escape.

I found it in weed. My weed guy that I found my first day in Salt Lake City led me to this Mexican gang. Yes, I managed to find the only Mexican gang in this Mormon state. I arranged for the leader of the gang to bring weed to me weekly and either leave it in my stash spot in my backyard or wrap it up to look like a gift or a package and leave it in my mailbox. I was getting my marijuana on schedule. I would pay him every month when I got my check.

We became real cool and I started hanging out with him and his brothers. We had a lot in common—weed and pit bulls. I loved dogs and they had a bunch of pit bulls, and I would just hang out with them and smoke and laugh. Once we started hanging out, I had access to all the weed I could smoke. I introduced them to blunts. They had been rolling their weed in E-Z Wider paper, and I showed them how to take a Phillies cigar and make a blunt. They never looked back at the corny joint after that. Those were my peoples.

They looked up to me. I was a little older than they were, so I became one of their OGs. They were also into guns. I also had a love of guns from the days my father used to take me hunting in the woods of Pennsylvania and western Jersey. My father and I would go coon hunting, rabbit hunting, squirrel hunting. Yeah, it was some real country shit. (We weren't *that* country because we never brought any of it back to eat.) But hunting with my father was one of those good memories that I held on to. It was one of the few times when he was relaxed. My grandmother also had a thing with guns and taught me how to shoot. She was really good.

I would go with my Mexican gang to pawnshops and buy .357 Magnums, shotguns, and rifles. We would go to the range, shoot guns, smoke weed, chase women, and party. I think I spent more time with them than I did practicing basketball.

Basketball was where I felt the least at home at this point. I felt all over again like that Prop 48 player in college. I wasn't playing. The coach wasn't feeling me. My teammates were frustrated with me, and I felt a lot of them had given up on me. I wanted out.

I figured if I did some crazy things, they would trade me. Some of the crazy things, though, happened by accident—such as the time I bought a rottweiler puppy while we were on the road and I tried to sneak him onto our plane. I figured it was a chartered plane, not commercial, so they shouldn't mind. I not only had to leave my puppy, but I got fined.

During a road trip to New York, we had to wait to play because a tennis match ran late in the Garden. I was hungry, so I asked one of the ball boys if he knew a good place to get something to eat. He told me about a sandwich joint nearby. I asked him to get me a turkey-and-cheese with lettuce, tomato, and mustard, some chips, and a soda. I gave him $50 and tipped him $20. I got in trouble for that.

We weren't supposed to eat right before a game, and I had a weight clause in my contract that I was having a hard time meeting. (Weed gives you the munchies, you know.) Somehow that story ended up in the *New York Daily News*. I was in the doghouse again.

But the big incident was in Houston. We were there to play the Rockets, and during warm-ups, I decided I would sit in with the house band and play the drums. It wasn't the actual warm-ups, but the shootaround, where the team was getting loose before we went back to the locker room for the game plan.

I noticed the band practicing and I was into music. I was shooting around with one of our guards, Calvin Duncan. Cleveland drafted him the same year as Patrick Ewing, Manute Bol, and Detlef Schrempf. He was traded to Utah the year I got there. We were cool.

"Do you think they would mind if I sat in with the band?" I asked him.

"Why not?" Calvin said. "Go ask them if you can."

He was egging me on. He thought I was a funny dude. I'm sure he never thought I would get in any real trouble.

Boy, was he wrong. I went over to the band. They were happy to let me sit in with them on the drums. I was going at it, having fun, when one of the coaches came over and told me that they needed to see me in the locker room. *Oh, brother!*

I basically got cursed out and hit with another fine. They couldn't threaten me with playing time because I wasn't getting that anyway. I figured what could be the harm in playing with the band when I wasn't playing in the games? What was I warming up for? I couldn't understand it then. (I do now.)

We lost to the Rockets and Coach Sloan tried to blame me for the loss, saying that all of that was a big distraction. *No, Hakeem Olajuwon and Clyde Drexler just busted your ass.*

When we got back from the road trip, I decided to stage a protest. If the Jazz were going to keep treating me like this, keeping me in the doghouse, fining me for dumb stuff, and not playing me, I was through with them. I stopped going to practice and team meetings and I just hung out with my peoples.

I was with my Mexican gang for days—I even missed a game. I got a room at a hotel. I watched the game on television from my hotel room. My attitude was "F the Jazz! Utah can kiss my black ass!"

I felt like the man with them. On the Utah Jazz I was the rookie, nobody. I was nothing. With my Mexican gang, I was important. I was the OG. It felt good. I was in a comfort zone around these guys because I didn't have to be perfect; I didn't have to live up to anything. They may have known I was a ballplayer, but it never came up. They loved hanging with Lou Bee because I was fun, I knew how to party, and I liked to get high—just as they did. I had more in common with them than I did with my teammates.

As my disappearance turned into days, people were now worried and looking for me. I told only one person—my stepbrother—where I was. He eventually told my stepfather. The snitch! Numa came and got me and drove me back home. He took the air out of the tires of my truck and thought that would keep me there.

I called my Mexican posse and they picked me up. We went back to their spot and smoked. I started bugging.

I asked the Mexicans to drive me to Houston. I didn't know how many hundreds of miles away it was. I just knew I wanted to go to Houston. What would I do when I got there? I would go talk to the coaches and management of the Rockets and ask them to trade for me. I thought I could convince them that I would be a great addition to their squad.

I don't know why I didn't just call Sal and ask him to negotiate something. I didn't understand how things worked, obviously. More than being high and out of my mind, I was ignorant. I thought if I made enough trouble, Utah would want to get rid of me and I could convince some team myself to let me play for them. I didn't understand the NBA to be this organization where everything is connected and that, by creating this drama, I made it so that no one wanted to get near me. I couldn't get traded if my life depended on it.

I was determined to get to Houston and that my Mexican friends would take me. But they said no. This was our first real disagreement. My boys were trying to talk me out of it. That's when I lost it.

They had this big hoopty. I don't remember the make and model, I just remember its being old and big. What I didn't know at the time was that their big hoopty had an industrial-size green garbage bag full of weed in the trunk. They weren't going to Houston not because they thought it was a bad idea. They weren't driving across state lines with a trunk full of weed and risk getting arrested. I know they were down for me, but I was asking too much.

I was yelling and screaming at them to take me, and I got into a fight with one of their uncles, who was trying to stop me. I grabbed his leg and it came off. I forgot he had a prosthetic leg, and I used his leg to smash out the windows of the car. I grabbed the keys out of the ignition and threw them across a field toward the Great Salt Lake. Then I started to walk. If they weren't going to drive me to Houston, I was going to walk there.

Now, it was the middle of the night. It was pitch-black. We're in the middle of nowhere. It was cold outside, but I'm hot. I took off my shirt—I guess that's where the naked stories got started—and I started walking.

I ended up in this empty lot. It was so dark, I couldn't see my hands in front of my face. I came across a Dumpster. I was lost. So I figured if I made some noise, someone would find me. I started pushing and lifting this heavy Dumpster and letting it drop. It sure did make a racket. I did this about ten times, then I heard what sounded like tires rolling over gravel. But I couldn't see where the sound was coming from until it got close to me.

It was a state trooper who didn't turn on his lights. I heard the ding-ding-ding when he opened his door and got out.

"Put your hands over your head," he barked at me.

Heck, I couldn't see my hands. But I knew he was pointing a gun at me. I could feel that. I put my hands over my head, and the next thing I felt were the cuffs going on. I was under arrest. Backup came shortly after. They didn't bother my Mexican friends. It took them a while to find their keys so they were still there. I told the cops they had nothing to do with it. Thank God for them, the cops never searched their car.

I was hauled down to the police station. Larry Miller, the owner of the Jazz, came and bailed me out. I went from jail to the psych ward, where I stayed for a few months under "evaluation."

Every day I had to meet with a counselor to talk about whether I was hearing voices. They had these cards and would ask me, "What does this picture look like?" It was a pain in the butt because I knew what they were going to ask me and I knew the answers they were looking for. In my head I was thinking I wasn't crazy and was asking, *Why are we doing this?*

I was definitely going through something, but I

couldn't identify what it was and how to stop it. But I knew inside I wasn't *really* crazy—not the kind of crazy they were telling me I was. So it was frustrating. I wasn't given an opportunity to communicate and honestly talk about it. They kept shoving pills down my throat.

Once they get you in a place like that, you're at their mercy. If you say certain things they don't like, they keep you longer. If you looked at them a certain way, they would tack on some extra time. It was like jail, only worse. I'd never experienced jail but I knew enough people who had. At least in jail you had time to spend with the general population to have some human interaction. They had me so medicated that I was cloudy most of the time.

I had no control over when I woke up, when I would eat, when I would sleep. Everything was on a schedule. They gave me pills for this and pills for that, pills to help me sleep, pills to make me feel nothing. Pills, pills, and more pills. I think I became more depressed being there than I was before I got there.

My mother would come to visit, but I didn't want to see her. I blamed her for my being there. I was looking for anyone and everyone to blame. I was also embarrassed. People were talking about me and I couldn't defend myself. I had done things to deserve to be put away like this.

I just knew that I was in the doghouse of everyone— the media, the coaches, the team, the town. Everybody was dogging me out. They had a field day. They were talking about me and making up stories. It was hard to not read the stuff. Facing the music was the hardest part. That was the driving factor in my even wanting to write a book. I wanted to finally tell what actually happened from my mouth in my way.

Nobody wanted to hear the truth. People wanted to make up their own stories. The only people who knew for sure what went down that whole week leading up to that incident were the Mexicans and me. And they weren't talking.

I was diagnosed with a range of mental illnesses ranging from manic depression to bipolar disease, from ADD to ADHD. I was committed for a couple of months, then I was shipped back to my home in Utah.

The first days at home were tough. I had had a lot of time to think while locked away—but they weren't clear thoughts. I was angry, hurt, and confused. Part of it might have been the medication I was on, but a lot of it was just how I was feeling at the time. I was mad at the world. I was playing the blame game—blaming everybody in my life for why I was in the situation I was in, and not looking at me. I blamed my mother. I felt that she should have or could have done something to stop me. She saw what was happening. We had a little squabble because I felt that she saw me falling into this crack and she wasn't trying to stop it or help me out of it. I felt that she was contributing to it. She wasn't working—none of my family was working—and it put an extra burden on me. I had to do it all. I blamed her for allowing me to do it all.

When I got home, none of those feelings had changed. Now I had to somehow put it all back together. I had to find a way to get it all back.

They prescribed about ten different pills that I had to take at different times of the day. While I was recovering, I started working out with a trainer to get back into shape and to try to focus on getting back to the team. I was still a member of the Jazz and yet still very much not a part of the team. They kept telling me I wasn't ready to come back. So I was home every day, trying to work through it.

One morning, I got up and decided I didn't want to do it anymore. I looked at these pill bottles lined up on my end table next to my bed. I had to take them every four hours. I decided to take all of them at once. I don't know if I was actually trying to kill myself, but I knew that I wanted what I was feeling to stop. I wanted it all to go away. I wanted to turn back the clock. I wanted to go back to when I was Luther Wright, the man in Jersey City, the president of Elizabeth High School, the star of Seton Hall University. I wanted to go back to the times when people were cheering for me and yelling out my name and asking for my autograph.

Now people were laughing at me and I was known as this crazy person. Every newspaper article was now talking about me negatively, not covering my basketball play anymore.

My mother must have sensed something was up because she came into my room to check on me, something she rarely did. She would usually give me my space. But this day she came in my room and found me on my bed with those empty pill bottles and called 911. I was rushed to the hospital and had my stomach pumped (that was very, very painful). Then I was shipped back to the mental hospital for another month's sentence.

This time, when I left the hospital, my mind was much clearer. The first time I was in, I was angry and still rebellious. This second stint broke me down. I had surrendered and I was tired of fighting against the grain.

I wanted a second chance. I wanted to prove myself. I needed to redeem myself. I believed that if I got a chance, I could prove that I could play in the league. I wasn't given that second chance, so who knows. We will never know what could have happened. Maybe I would have been retiring just now, and it hurts.

I left the hospital optimistic. I knew I was turning the corner in a good way. In the days leading up to my release I had decided that I would work out and get ready to be a part of the Utah Jazz. Even if I didn't get to play this season, I would still be a part of the team. I had an epiphany that I needed to do what they were paying me to do and suck it up. I had made a decision.

Unfortunately, so had the Jazz.

I went back to the team ready. I went through training camp and everything seemed to be going well. It wasn't in Hawaii, but it was nice and relaxing and I was getting back into that basketball routine.

The team seemed ready for me, too. That first day, all of my teammates were patting me on the back and telling me that they were glad to see me.

"Welcome back, Big Lou," they were saying.

I was feeling pretty good. We went through training camp, then we were back to the Delta Center preparing for our first preseason game. I had a good, hard practice, and when I got home from that, I got a call from Sal.

"Luther, they are releasing you," he said. "They want you out of there."

What? How could that be? Everybody was so nice and everything was going so well. Then I started thinking about how phony everybody was. No one said a word or even hinted that it was going to go down like that. They were so smooth with it.

"Start packing up," Sal said. "I'll help you move back to New Jersey. We'll work something out."

I believed things would work out. Their releasing me hit me like a ton of bricks. It was over. I felt that my world was crashing around me. No more basketball? No more cheering fans? No more special treatment? I couldn't see any options. I didn't have a plan. What was I going to do now? Who was I?

Almost as bad as hearing I would be released was then having to tell my mother and stepfather and brother and sister. I had to tell my family that I had failed them. It was weird because while I was feeling as if I had let them down, I was also feeling that they had let me down. I was mad at them for basically living off me and not contributing. Always taking and never giving.

I moved them to Utah to make my life easier. But that didn't happen. Now I was feeling as if I'd brought them out there for nothing. I uprooted their lives and I wouldn't be able to keep taking care of them. I didn't want to have to tell them that the party was over. At the same time, I was relieved to tell them that the gravy train had hit a wall. It was a confusing time for me.

While I felt responsible for my family, I was doing everything to undercut their security. I was in Utah to play basketball professionally. And I acted spoiled and immature and irresponsible. I had it all. And I threw it away.

Now I had to pack everything and everybody back up and move back to Jersey? We didn't have a home there or anything. We had no place to go. I would have to start from scratch.

I was completely lost.

14) THE CRACK OF DAWN

stayed in Utah, packing up my things and getting rid of my home and possessions. It wasn't nice and it wasn't cool. I didn't have to say a word to my mother. She knew. You didn't need to be a rocket scientist to know that I had got the boot from Utah. She would have to find a place for us to live in New Jersey and start putting the pieces back together. She left with my step-father and brother.

I kept thinking how I should never have brought them out to Utah in the first place and how I let everybody down. It's still hard talking about it to this day. So many emotions are tied to leaving Utah. It wasn't just an end to my basketball career, it seemed like the end of me.

It was a big adjustment for everybody. Imagine living the life, not worrying about bills or money or anything. They got what they wanted whenever they wanted. No bill was ever late. Imagine getting the VIP treatment every place you go. Imagine having it all, and then in just two short years losing it all.

My world was crashing around me, and I couldn't stop it. I was looking at my family settling back in New Jersey, nobody working, acting as if everything were fine. And it was for them. Everything was still being paid for, money was still coming in, but I was miserable.

I felt that I was being used—from the Jazz right down to my family. I was talking. I had been saying a lot through my acting out and taking drugs, but no one was paying attention. People didn't understand what I was going through not playing and being in Utah. Then you know the saying—when it rains, it pours. I started getting hit with a bunch of women claiming they were having my baby. It was definitely the wrong time for me to hear that.

All of these thoughts were swirling in my head at once.

Then they diagnosed me with these sicknesses. I was crazy, right? At least that's what everybody was saying. In a way, that crazy thing let me off the hook. I could say, "Hey, I couldn't help myself. I'm crazy." I didn't have to take full responsibility for what I did to put my-self in this situation. I had a diagnosis to lean on. I had a bunch of pills to take to prove it. I wasn't wrapped too tight. But I knew in my heart that I wasn't truly crazy. It was an easy excuse.

When I got back to Jersey, Sal talked about getting me something overseas. He had some connections. He could place me on a team immediately. But I didn't want to play overseas. Utah was tough enough. I couldn't imagine being in a foreign country with the way I was thinking about things. He tried to get me up and out of it, but by the time I got back to Jersey I was so depressed and feeling so bad, I didn't want to do a thing—but get high.

My mother found a house in our old neighborhood in Irvington. I moved in with her, my sister, and her kids. My mother and my stepfather were on the outs and in the middle of breaking up, so he got his own place. I missed having Numa around. He was a good guy and definitely provided some stability in our home.

Those first few weeks back in Jersey I didn't want to talk to anybody. I didn't want to do anything. I must have slept for two weeks straight. All I did was lie around the house, smoking weed.

My mother started in on me to get out of the house and do something. So I did. I left the house and started getting high for real. I started smoking coke heavily.

I lived in a neighborhood where it was easy to find drugs. If you wanted to get something, everybody knew where to go. That was easy. And finding people to smoke with? That was easy, too. Finding places to smoke? Easy. You could even get a crack pipe from the local bodega.

That was easy. So it was all too easy for me to smoke coke every day.

Smoking made me feel a whole lot better. The weed made me sleep, the coke made me numb. While I was doing it, I didn't think about anything but feeling that high.

All of the medication they prescribed was adding to the crazy. It had me putting on weight, and the combination of the ten pills with the weed and the cocaine wasn't good. I was mixing the prescription drugs with the illegal drugs.

I hear this all the time: "You were an athlete, how could you use drugs?"

It's complicated. I can't say that even I understand it myself.

I tried drugs the first time partly to fit in, partly due to peer pressure. But a big part was curiosity. You wonder, what will happen if you do it? Will it affect you? Will you *really* get high? And what will that feel like?

You also think that you're different, that you're special, that somehow it won't have the same impact on you.

It started off for me with marijuana, and even with that, it was a curiosity thing. I would hear people talk about how they smoked a joint. I would say to myself, *What's a joint?* I found out when I was sixteen. I won't say who introduced me to it. It was a fellow basketball player, and I remember it as if it were last night.

I was in Plainfield, New Jersey, in somebody's house right after AAU practice, and I had had the worst practice I ever had in my life. We were talking about the practice the whole way to Plainfield. When we got there, somebody said, "I got some weed, man. You with it, Lou?"

"I'm down for whatever," I said. "I'm from Jersey City. I'm from Chilltown. I'm with whatever."

Like they say, curiosity kills the cat? Well, I was that cat. I can't blame anyone but me. I decided to take that first hit of that joint. I did that, no one else. But that's been my life. I either made good choices or I made bad choices. That's life for everyone, I guess.

When I made good choices, they were really good—NBA, $5 million deal (that I'm still eating off of), turning to God. But when I made bad choices . . . drug addict, homeless, losing my toes and my mind.

They say in recovery that one time is too many and a thousand times is never enough.

That was my one time and it was too many. I started smoking weed pretty regularly in high school. I graduated to cocaine in college. Once again, a teammate turned me on to it. Once again, like a dummy, I had to try it and see for myself.

The drugs seemed to fit in with everything else. There was basketball, and with that came the parties and the social life. You're popular when you play basketball, so you get invited to all of the parties and you get into the clubs for free. You're a VIP. When you're partying, there is the drinking. So I used to drink, too. But I didn't like drinking as much as I liked smoking weed. Weed made me feel mellower. I didn't really like how alcohol made me feel.

So there was the partying, the smoking, the dibbing and dabbing, and the women. I treated women the way I treated all of it—fun, social, for my pleasure only. Then I would move on. I never saw women as people back then. They were just there, like the music and the drugs, for my entertainment.

But cocaine, cocaine was beyond social. The bond there was hard to break. By the time I graduated to crack, it was a wrap. I wasn't thinking about anything or anyone. It was just that crack and me, and when I didn't have crack, all I was thinking about was how I was going to get some. Crack came before everything else in my life. With crack I could totally tune out and not feel. Weed took the edge off, but as far as emotions go, crack was like being put under for surgery.

I had a lot of things I was running from and not wanting to feel, and crack was the perfect medicine for what ailed me. I didn't want to feel the pain.

When it finally started to sink in that I wouldn't be playing basketball anymore, I started smoking crack hard. Everybody was telling me how I fucked up. I wanted to fight every time someone said something to me or shook his head and looked at me as if I were pitiful.

There isn't enough time in the day to explain it. The regret is so deep.

All most people see is the money I threw away. But I threw away so much more. I threw away the opportunity to be great, to be the one that they talk about long after I'm gone. I was a raw talent project and I didn't develop because I didn't have the right frame of mind, I didn't have the discipline, the dedication, the determination, the right people in my corner. I should have been more. I should have listened.

Karl Malone and John Stockton were telling me, "We need you, man." But I tuned them out.

The former Jazz center Mark Eaton was in my ear, too. He had retired and was telling me what a great opportunity this was for me, and it was. It upsets me that I blew that.

Sal kept coming at me with different opportunities, but none of them was in the NBA. If it wasn't the NBA, I didn't want to play. It would feel like a major step backward. As if I hadn't already taken a huge step backward. I couldn't see that I could work my way back to the NBA. I couldn't see them giving me another chance. So why even try to get back by playing overseas or in the CBA or some other league? Why play at all if I couldn't play in the NBA? I gave up.

I smoked and smoked and smoked until all I could feel was the desire to keep getting high.

All I wanted was the next hit.

15) FALLING THROUGH THE CRACKS

Escape came in the form of music and crack cocaine. At the height of my getting high, it would not be unusual to find me in a club near the deejay booth. I might even ask to do a set. It would be one of the few moments of sobriety I might have in weeks. Being in that booth, spinning those records, seeing the people dance, gave me that feeling that I missed of the ball going through the hoop. It was the appreciation that I couldn't find any place else but on the basketball court or in a crowd while playing music.

Even when I was homeless, I would end up in a club from time to time or a local bar. It was one of the few things that connected me to something normal. Being in a club around music, around the turntables, made me forget my problems. It was almost like a drug for me.

I would go to a dollar store and get a rag, a bar of soap, and go to McDonald's and freshen up in their bathroom. I would go to the Laundromat and wash my clothes or go stay with a girl for a couple days and get cleaned up for a minute. Until the crack called. Then I was gone.

I was just using people back then. Even going to the clubs, which was definitely about the music, was also about getting my buzz on for free.

I was still Luther Wright. When I came into a club, people who remembered me from back in the day would show me love. People would buy me drinks all night. Liquor, as I mentioned, was not my drug of choice. It became a substitute when I didn't have money for crack. Bacardi 151.

One night, I downed six double shots at a bar in Newark. Before I knew anything, I was vomiting in the mop bucket, tore up. Everybody was still dancing. I got myself together and got right back into partying. Homeless and partying and enjoying my independence.

I was a survivor of another kind.

While my family lived in a nice house in Irvington, my new home in Jersey was on Ellis Avenue off Springfield Avenue in Irvington. I found an abandoned house among a row of abandoned houses where I would spend most of my nights when I was living on the street.

At first I stayed with my mother after returning from Utah. But that lasted less than a month before I had enough. It was noisy and crowded in that house and I couldn't do what I wanted to do because my moms was always on me. She was always there, asking me questions.

In true Lou Bee fashion, I decided that if I was going to hit rock bottom, I was going to go all the way. I spent days in bed, sleeping, smoking, and eating. I didn't feel like doing anything and definitely didn't feel like being bothered. Every day my mother would ask me what I was going to do, harassing me.

"Are you high?" she kept asking me.

Not yet. But if you keep asking me, I will be, I would be thinking, but I would never say a word. My mother threatened to call the cops and have me committed again if I didn't snap out of it. So I left. I got up one morning, I think it was a Tuesday, walked out, and never went back. I wasn't being committed again. That wasn't happening.

I'd rather be on the streets doing exactly what I wanted to do when I wanted to do it than to hear her mouth—or anyone else's, which is why I didn't stay long with any girl. I would be with a girlie a couple of days, the nagging would start, and I was gone.

Ellis Avenue off Springfield Avenue in Irvington. In the summertime I would sleep on the porch in a sleeping bag I had found. When it got cold, I would go inside and start a fire to keep warm.

This house wasn't just abandoned, it was dilapidated. I got in through a back window that was open. I had to be careful because the steps were missing. It was dangerous. But I didn't care.

I tried to stay out of sight and was low-key. The only people who knew I was there were the people on the block. Drug dealers and other junkies. Some local cops knew I was there, too. They, too, knew me from back in the day, and sometimes they would stop by and drop off clothes and food and even money. That was my spot at night.

During the day, I got my hustle on. After my monthly check was done, which was usually within a week, I would go out early and start begging—nickel-and-diming people for money to get enough to buy a nickel of coke, which was $5.

I would ask people for a dollar, fifty cents, a quarter, anything they could spare. Most people gave me a dollar, some even gave me a whole five. That was a good day. I picked a good spot. A McDonald's was on one corner, a Popeyes on another. A Subway and a Dunkin' Donuts were right there, too. I had plenty of people to hit up for cash. I knew all of the managers at those spots, so I would get free food, too. Some would let me sit there and eat and enjoy my food.

I turned it into a game, into a competition. All of these other crackheads were out there, begging and robbing and trying to get high, but I had to be the best. I had these little victories, such as if I could get my $5 before ten o'clock. I would set these little goals for my-self. How much money could I get in an hour or two hours. I used my celebrity to get money from people. I did anything I had to do to get that money so I could get high.

I would get my drugs and go back to my *abandon-minium* to get high.

Irvington has a lot of abandoned places, so I picked one that was in the middle of the block where I wouldn't be bothered much. It was equipped with candles, a flash-light, and rats. I had a pit bull that I "borrowed" from a cousin and never returned. I loved dogs and I asked if I could walk him. I just never went back with him. That was my companion. He protected me on those streets.

But if I could have sold him for money to buy crack, I would have. A crackhead is only interested in getting more crack, by any means necessary.

The few times I went into a recovery facility (I did this about three times during my time on the streets), I used it for the free meals, to have some sex (you can always find someone to have sex with), and to get some rest. You don't get much rest on the streets; you always have to be on guard.

Being in a recovery facility was a vacation for me. When I felt like getting my fix, I left and went right back on the streets, getting high. The memories of being molested. The memories of what I lost in basketball. The lost fame and fortune. The missed opportunities. But it was mostly the unresolved issues of my childhood. The molesters, the rapists that I never confronted. The feelings about it that I never confronted. I was a mess.

I was luckier than most because I actually had steady money coming in every month. I knew that I would be able to pay for my habit. Under the contract that Sal negotiated, I would get a lump sum every month for twenty years. That lump sum was about $15,000 when I first got out of the league. But my mother took over my money. While I was committed to the mental hospital in Utah, my mother got power of attorney.

I don't know what she did, but by the time I sobered up, that lump sum had dwindled down to $1,000 a month. It was so crazy. I think she borrowed against the annuity. Again, I don't know because I wasn't paying attention.

When I was getting high, I just cared about getting my money and buying my drugs. I didn't have a bank account, so I had my check routed to a local furniture store in Newark that also cashed checks called the Credit Doctors. I know now they took a hefty fee to cash my check. When I was halfway sober, I would have them hold back half or more of the money for me later. I knew if I took all of it, I would spend all of it in just a few days getting high. I would buy so much in those first days after getting my check that I would often pass out from using too much.

That's how I was living—for three or four days, I was the man, I was rich. But when the party was over, I was back to the streets. That would mean that the rest

of the month, I would have to get creative. I would usually stand outside a McDonald's or Popeyes or Dunkin'
Donuts and beg. So many people knew me from my
days playing at Elizabeth, St. Anthony, and Seton Hall.
I would get a lecture from time to time: "Luther, man,
why are you out here like this?" "You were in the
NBA"—*as if I don't know that*—"what happened to
you?" I would listen and in my mind I'd be saying, *Yeah,
yeah, yeah, just give me some money so I can get high.*

When the begging wasn't enough—and it was never
enough—I'm embarrassed to say that I would steal. If
I saw somebody on a bike and he was dumb enough to
leave it for a minute without a chain, I would take it.
The toaster, the microwave, the cable box—if I had an
opportunity to steal it, I would. You wouldn't want to
invite me into your home because you felt sorry for me
because I would steal your stuff and be out to get high.
That was me.

That *is* me. It's still a part of me. I say that because
I know that man is still inside me. He's there. Some
people let themselves off the hook by saying that when
they were doing crazy things, it wasn't them. It was
somebody else. But I know that it was me. That man
is asleep. I knocked him out—hopefully for good. But
if I don't keep that image of myself in front of me, if I
don't acknowledge that at any point that man (who is
me) can wake up again, then I can't fully recover. I have
to remind myself that he's there waiting for me to slip,
waiting for me to get weak, waiting for me.

If you forget where you came from and you act as if you never did those things and you don't thank God for delivering you, you're doomed to repeat them. You're setting yourself up to go back there. I'm not going back.

But back then, I surrounded myself with drugs and people who did drugs. I hung out in drug areas. Drug addicts, junkies, and alcoholics were my friends. Some of them I would hit off with money or drugs at the first of the month when I got my check. I had their back.

No one could get me to stop. Nothing could, either. Not even when I lost my front teeth, which came out about a year after I hit the streets. I had an infection in my gums and they had to be pulled. A person can't take care of himself on the streets. I didn't brush my teeth most days. You can't take a bath. You don't have a bed, so you're putting this wear and tear on your body. I was trying to camp out in the hood pretty much. That's how I looked at it. As if I were a survivor man, and instead of being in the woods or some remote jungle, I was in the urban jungle.

This jungle was eating me up—bit by bit. Literally.

Jheri curls were in at the time. This is me in
5th grade—and I was already 6′4″!

Left: In position to grab a rebound at Elizabeth High.

Below: With my baby sister Courtney—she had just graduated from middle school. God rest her soul! Her graduation was the same day as one of my New Jersey Nets workouts.

Above: Happy birthday to me! At Seton Hall, age twenty-one. Finally legal, but still a big kid.

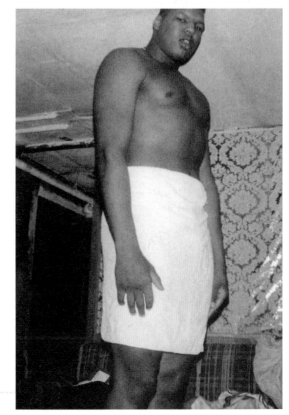

Right: Not quite fitting in my own house! My head almost touched the ceiling!

Agent Sal, Willis Reed, and Mom at a New Jersey Nets workout.

In London, representing the U.S.A. in the Junior Olympics.

Above: Draft Day with Mom and Numa. I should look happier, right?

Right: My official NBA Draft photo.

Draft Day in Detroit. Dean Bradley, Mom, and Numa. I wasn't the tallest player drafted that year!

My first training camp in Hawaii! Living the life of an NBA baller.

Luther Wright (Utah Jazz) guarding Shaquille O'Neal (Orlando Magic).

GETTY IMAGES

Taking a free throw for the Utah Jazz.

GETTY IMAGES

I am the father! My little girl,
Paris, age 3.

Me and my blushing bride.
I love this woman!

One year clean!
Taking recovery
one day at a time.

16) FOULED OUT

t was December 22, 2004—a couple of days before Christmas, but that didn't mean a thing to me. Christmas, birthdays, no holidays had anything for me. My days were spent with one thing on my mind—getting high. I was annoyed that I had this issue that I couldn't ignore any longer.

The pain was so bad when I made my way down to UMDNJ the first time, I don't know how I did it. But I made it. I didn't have on a shoe. I had on a sock or a makeshift sock out of paper towels or rags or whatever I could get to wrap around my foot, which was pretty numb and stinking.

When I got to the hospital, though, they acted as if they didn't want to treat me and that nothing was seriously wrong. They gave me some painkillers and I kept it moving. But in a few days, things started getting worse. I noticed that my toes had turned black and they were starting to smell. I could hardly walk and the pain was so bad I couldn't take it.

I had been on the streets on and off for seven years at this point. This was my new court. This was my new life. Smoking crack, stealing and begging for money to buy crack, finding places to smoke crack, and enjoying the short time that I was high on crack. Then it would start all over again. When I got too tired, I'd find a place to rest— with my mother, a woman, or even rehab. But it wouldn't be for long. I was more comfortable on the streets with my drug "friends" than I was with sober people.

There was always some drama on the streets.

I had somehow managed to squeeze into the back of an abandoned hatchback car on Ellis Avenue. I had been scoping it out for a few days. It was parked next to my abandonminium, which had just about caved in on my head the night before. I needed shelter.

It was getting cold and the porch where I had been sleeping wasn't going to work. So I checked the door of this car. It was unlocked and I got in. I started smoking and I guess sparks from the match ignited some oil or something in the back of this car. It all went up in flames. The fire got big quickly.

I don't know to this day how I got out. It happened so fast. I was just lucky. It was raining cats and dogs and I was running up the street like a crazy man. People were looking at me like "Oh, he's just high. He must have got a good one there. Look at him!"

Things were unraveling for me on the streets. The car fire was the first close call, but not the last.

I had been walking around in the same shoes for more than a year. They were worn-out and didn't give me much support and my feet were hurting. I was wearing a size twenty, but I actually wear a size twenty-two. I had been wearing shoes that were too small for years because something in my mind said wearing a size twenty-two would make me a bigger freak than I already felt. I could get away with squeezing my feet into expensive sneakers and shoes that would eventually mold to my feet, but not these.

My feet were hurting all of the time. After the car fire, I tried to make my home back on the porch of that house on Ellis Avenue. I found some blankets and I had that sleeping bag and I huddled up in a corner. I took off my shoes and put them to the side. I fell asleep on the porch and when I woke up, one of my shoes was gone. I guess as a joke someone came by and took one shoe. So I was walking around with one shoe because I couldn't get a size twenty or twenty-two at a thrift store. Most of my shoes I had to special order.

The shoe wasn't that important to me. Getting high was more important. I could have a shoe or not have a shoe. It didn't matter. That's how crazy my life had become.

It was winter and it was getting colder and colder. I was looking for a spot to smoke. I found an abandoned truck parked on the block. Irvington's got a lot of abandoned things. I took off my one shoe and my socks. I passed out. When I came to, it felt as if my feet were frozen.

I was like "Oh, no." I looked down and noticed that my two little toes on my right foot were blue. I kept saying, "I got to go to the hospital." I went to the hospital and they looked at them, but they discharged me. I didn't have insurance or Medicaid or cash. So they put me back out on the street. I knew they weren't going to do anything for me. They wrapped up my foot in some gauze and bandages, and I was good to go.

I spent enough time in there to thaw out and I was back on my hunt for drugs. I felt pain in my foot, but I blamed it on the cold. The pain got worse and worse, to the point where I couldn't walk across the street. It was so excruciating I was screaming. I made it back to the hospital.

The doctor said if I hadn't come when I did, they might have had to cut off my whole foot. At least through the crack haze I had enough sense to get some help.

This time they didn't turn me away. They admitted me. I remember being rushed onto a gurney and into an operating room. They didn't put me under; they just numbed me from the waist down. I could hear everything. I was full of painkillers but I was more sober than I had been in years.

I could hear them, each toe as they hit the metal pan. *Ping. Ping.* That's when reality set in. *You've only got eight toes. For real, for real.*

When I left the hospital later that day, I was missing two toes. When they first said *amputation*, it still didn't register. Not until I heard the toes hit the pan did I know that I had to make some changes. I'm not sure if I made a deal then with the Man upstairs, but I know it was the first time in a long time that He and I had a conversation. That talk went something like this: "I'm tired. I'm ready to listen to what You have to tell me."

That talk didn't last long, though.

When they released me from the hospital, I took the bus to my mother's house. She was going to take care of me, nurse me back to health. But that crack was still calling. I still needed to get high—especially after the painkillers they gave me at the hospital wore off. Getting high had been the most important thing in my life for a few years, and just because I had surgery to remove my toes, I couldn't see that changing.

Not more than eight hours after getting out of the hospital, I was back on the streets. I left my mother's house and made my way on crutches down to my spot on Twentieth Street between Seventeenth and Eighteenth avenues.

The crack house was three stories, white and dingy

on a bad block with a bunch of abandoned buildings and houses in need of repair. This one was being renovated. But they were slow doing it and hadn't worked on it in weeks. People were squatting there. The people who were paid to watch the house to keep the riffraff out had done just the opposite. For a little bit of dough, they let a few of us in to get high.

This place was like a haven, a place I could smoke in peace. It was the closest thing I had found to home in a while. There were a few chairs, a couch, even a big-screen TV in the living room. Nobody bothered me. I would even share some of my crack as payback for the peace.

I bought my stuff, went inside, sat on the couch, and laid my crutches down. I put the rock in my pipe and lit it up. As I took my first hit, I looked down and saw blood seeping from my bandaged foot, which was covered by a white sock. The blood was really flowing freely, turning the whole sock red.

I got scared because it wouldn't stop bleeding. I put down the pipe, got my crutches, and made my way back to the hospital. The doctor didn't say much. If you don't have insurance, you get treated like an African with a fly in your eye. They just want to get you out of there as quickly as possible. I knew what time it was and I didn't take it personally. It's business. They changed the bandage and gave me bus fare to get home. On that bus ride home, I made a decision. No more crack.

I decided that I would smoke just weed. It wasn't as bad.

I went along like this for a few months and everything was fine. I was getting back to normal with my routine. Instead of getting crack, I was getting my weed and going to my spot and smoking. One day, I was hanging with my boys. (I know now they weren't really my boys, but just people I did drugs with.) I remember it as if it were yesterday.

It was April 6, 2005, a nice, sunny, cool spring day. One of my boys was celebrating his birthday. He used to smoke PCP. I was smoking a blunt and he was smoking his PCP. After a few hits, he seemed to get stuck. I had seen this happen before, but now for some reason it truly hit me. I mean the dude was on his porch and wanted to go into the house but couldn't. He couldn't move.

I just sat there watching him. It was amazing. Everybody was laughing, but I didn't think it was funny. It was pretty sad. I passed the blunt and went back into the house.

"I'm done," I said. "This is it."

I went home to my mother's house, which was my first step back into the real world. I knew in my mother's house I couldn't get high. But that house was stressing me out, making me want to go back to the streets. My mother was there, but so was my sister, her boyfriend, and her three kids. It was a madhouse—lots of fighting and noise. I called my cousin May May and told her to come get me.

"I have to get out of this house," I told her.

May took me to a halfway house where I could stay until I got on my feet. That is where I started to get involved with recovery. I knew I didn't want to get high anymore, and I also knew that I needed help. The urge was so powerful (still is sometimes) that I couldn't do this by myself cold turkey.

Of course, I knew about Narcotics Anonymous and Alcoholics Anonymous, but I never took any of that seriously. I had been in "recovery" and treatment centers before. I had even checked into rehab facilities for months. I just couldn't relate to it. I mean, who looks at himself or herself as an addict? It all seemed corny. I knew I couldn't see myself saying, "Hi, my name is Luther and I'm an addict." Nah.

I had a problem with that because I was holding on to my pride. Picture that. I had lost my career, lost my lifestyle, lost a couple of toes and a few teeth, yet I cared about how things looked? I guess I wanted to hold on to something. But that was the last thing I had to let go of—my pride.

I was a crackhead. I had to look at myself, admit it, and decide to change.

It's funny, you always hear people talk about crackheads, but I never had an image of what a crackhead looked like. Growing up, I was too busy playing basketball to even notice. I didn't have the time to run the streets and do some of the things other kids my age were doing because my life was filled with basketball.

So I didn't know to fear ever becoming a crackhead.

Yet, here I was, a full out-and-out crackhead, and I didn't care.

Whitney Houston hit the nail on the head in her 2009 interview with Oprah. When you're doing your drug of choice, you aren't thinking about anything except getting rid of that pain. You are trying to hide the pain, and the only way to hide the pain is to get high.

Some people snorted it, others cooked it, I smoked it. I laced my weed with cocaine and smoked it. It was the escape. When there wasn't weed or cocaine, I would drink.

I just wanted the pain to go away.

I was ready now to get at the root of the pain. Maybe the amputation was the catalyst. But I know inside that if that hadn't happened, something else would have. If it were not the toes, something else would have woken me up. I know it. God was going to get my attention one way or another.

I entered a recovery facility for real this time.

I just got tired. I was tired of living like that.

In recovery you're surrounded by other recovering addicts. You learn from others, and what I learned is that the best way to break this habit is to just do it. I went to meetings and listened. It wasn't about me. It was about going and not feeling threatened and being on guard. It was about taking the journey. If you cut yourself short halfway through the journey, you're wasting your time. I used to cut myself short. I wouldn't take it seriously. I wouldn't identify with being an addict. "Hi, my name is Luther and I'm an addict"? Nah. I hated the sound of that and what that meant. My pride wouldn't let me say that the other times I checked into rehab. I wasn't trying to identify with being a dope fiend.

It's a bad thing to be an addict. But being a *recovering* addict is a blessing. I learned that this time in rehab. As a recovering addict, not only are you going to help yourself, but you can also help others. As simple as "one day at a time" sounds, that's the struggle. Temptation is all around us. You can get caught out there so easily. It only takes one time. You have to approach it as if any day you can get caught. Once you're serious about that, you can have success. Once you admit to yourself that you're weak and you can't do it by yourself, you can have success. Once you admit that you are what you are—an addict—you can have success.

It's not any one program that does the trick. It's you. It's not the program, it's the people around you. It's like basketball. You can't win a game by yourself. As great as LeBron James is, he can't win a thing by himself.

Part of it is the group, the sponsor, the team of people who are there to support you through your recovery. But the other part is you. When you're not with your group, you're not with your sponsor, what choices do you make? What do you do when you end up in a bar at a birthday party and someone buys you a drink? You have a choice. Me, I leave. I have to excuse myself and keep it moving. But I have a choice in that moment.

The hardest part for me this time around is staying

clean. Because I want to use again. I can't lie. I want it sometimes. I am tempted. But I make a choice not to. I think about it, and I know I can't go back. For me to keep it moving, I have to leave it in the past.

I feel good that when I'm weak or struggling, I have options. We make it hard. But recovery is easy. You just can't use. You have to keep your recovery in front of you. Don't get caught up in your stinking thinking because your best thinking got you where you're at.

Don't try to fool anybody.

Somebody told me if it doesn't come out in the wash, it will come out in the rinse. Don't come to a meeting trying to share and you just relapsed. People know. I can always tell when people do that. People think they're getting over, but everybody can see it. So you're not fooling anybody.

The first thing they teach you in recovery—the one thing that you have to get or you will never get better—is to accept that you *are* an addict. You have to admit to yourself and the world that you have a problem.

Even to this day—and I count every single day sober as one more day because it truly is just one day at a time—if I run into people who drink or smoke or use drugs, I will tell them that I'm an addict and if they want to drink and do drugs, I will leave. I need them to know my struggle, and I also need to get away from that environment. By telling them, I hold them accountable and I hold myself accountable.

I don't test God. I know me. I know that when it

comes to using, one time is too many and a thousand times is never enough. I understand that. I also understand that the Lord giveth and the Lord taketh away. But He will restore you.

Basketball was a blessing. I could have fun doing something and get paid. Now I have to work for my money. As a player, I just had to do what the coaches told me to do. Now as a coach, I have to prepare plays, study tapes, recruit players, come up with game plans. I actually have to work. But I look forward to it because it sure beats what I had been doing when I was out on the streets. Yes, I lost a career many would die for, but I found myself.

I was hurting about not being able to play basketball. Everybody was telling me how I fucked up. I wanted to fight the next person who said that. There isn't enough time in the day to explain what I was going through. All people were seeing was the millions of dollars. They didn't understand the dedication, the sacrifice, the discipline, it takes to actually play in the NBA. There is a reason why so few basketball players make it there.

I was just a raw talent project and I didn't develop. I didn't develop because I didn't have the right frame of mind. I didn't have the discipline, the dedication, the determination, the right people in my corner. I should have been more. I should have listened. I should have. But I didn't.

Now all I have to hold on to are those memories.

But more than what I should have been, I am grateful for what I am. What I am today is a man in recovery.

I still go to meetings. I try to go once a week, not because I'm struggling with anything but just to stay humble, because one slip can put me right back there. I go because you never know when that day will come when you fall right back into it. I know it can happen.

Today, I have no problem. Every time I go to a recovery meeting, I proudly say, "I'm Luther and I'm an addict."

17) YOU ARE . . . NOT
THE FATHER!

As part of my recovery and being clean and sober and spiritually led, I had to clean up the messes I had made over the past five-plus years. I couldn't fix my basketball career; that was done. But I could fix my life, and I had a lot of cleaning up to do.

One of the casualties of my behavior were the children I had across the country. As you know, I had a lot of girlfriends, and several of them told me I had their child. I had been paying child support for most of them, but one of the things I wanted to do and make sure of was that I wasn't just meeting a financial obligation. If

I had a child out there, I needed to know that child, and that child needed to know he or she had a daddy.

And if I had been paying child support for a child, I needed to make sure that child was mine!

At NBA rookie orientation, they told us basic stuff, such as when you're with a woman, no means no. It seemed like common sense—but quite a few guys got caught up in rape cases. They talked about how we should protect ourselves, use condoms, be careful of groupies, and don't get trapped, so that we wouldn't get caught up in paternity suits.

I should have been paying close attention to that.

I never thought about wearing condoms and all of that, I'm embarrassed to say. The girls were pretty and I felt it was their responsibility to take care of all of that. I couldn't imagine a girl *trying* to get pregnant. How naive was I?

My junior year at Seton Hall, the young lady I was dealing with, whom I met at Club Zanzibar in Newark, told me she was pregnant.

I said, "Okay, I have to go pro."

That was definitely one of the factors in my decision. I might have stayed at Seton Hall had I not been hit with that. I was growing tired of the whole college thing and was dreaming about the money and the freedom anyway. But with a baby coming, my decision was made easier.

The baby coming and my mother's health, and the numerous distractions, put me in pro mode. I felt that if I made a couple of extra dollars, everything would be fine.

I was actually excited about becoming a father—especially having a son. I was happy because I knew I would be able to take care of the kid. I was all in. I was buying baby clothes. I was on campus and she was at home.

When the time came, she called me and told me she was heading to the hospital. Her water had broken. My mom and I went to the hospital in New Brunswick, New Jersey. We were both in the room when the baby came.

When the baby came out, I said, "Oh, shit, look at that!"

My mother elbowed me and told me to chill out.

It was a boy!

After the baby came, things took a turn for the worse—for me and my girlfriend. Things started to be revealed that I hadn't noticed before. While we were dating, she seemed to have a lot of kids around. I thought she was babysitting these kids. She told me they were her sister's kids. After the doctor delivered my son, I remembered the doctor saying to her, "I don't want to see you here like this anymore. You've had enough."

I didn't catch it right then. But my mother caught it. Moms told me I needed to find out what was up. I confronted her and she came clean. *All* of those other kids were hers! That was reason enough to leave. We broke up after the baby came. And after I got drafted and moved on to Utah, she was completely out of my life. I was paying child support, though.

I found out about a year later she was pregnant again. I'm just glad I wasn't around for her to pin that birth on me.

When I got clean and sober, that first incident with her, which happened before all hell broke loose in my life, made me start to do some investigation into the other children I supposedly had. I contacted my lawyer in 2006, and he ordered paternity tests on all of my children.

That DNA stuff hadn't been on my radar.

My biggest fear had been being a deadbeat dad. That wouldn't be a good look. I wanted to make sure I did the right thing by my kids. You could call me a crackhead, you could even call me crazy, but I never wanted to be called a deadbeat dad. So I tried to be real good about that part of my life.

But once we started with the paternity tests, I realized how much I was out of it. The lawyer I hired to sift through this drama made all of the women who claimed to have children by me get a paternity test. It turned into a couple of bad episodes of a *Maury Povich/Jerry Springer* TV show.

The first baby, the results were in, and I was . . . *not* the father! That meant for thirteen years I was paying child support and taking care of a child that wasn't mine.

Not only had the mother lied that this was her first child, but that baby wasn't even mine. I'd named him Luther Shaheed Wright. I gave him the name Shaheed after one of my boys that had passed away. I even had little Luther's birthday tattooed on my arm. Like Lamont Sanford, I was a big dummy!

I knew the mother was a liar after I found out about the other babies. But I learned that *everything* she'd told me from day one was a lie. She told me she was in the service. That was a lie. She told me she wasn't in the service anymore because she was run over by a tank. That was a lie. She said her spleen got crushed and she couldn't have kids. That was a lie.

I was clueless. Maybe I was smoking too much weed to see clearly. I'm not blaming it on the alcohol, but the weed might have been the culprit. I was totally duped.

I felt that I wasted my time, energy, and a lot of money, not to mention a tattoo.

I never thought about DNA. The type of man I am, if I was sleeping with you and you said you were having a baby, then I was the father. That was it.

When I found out that Luther Jr. wasn't my child, Miss X, as I will call her, didn't apologize. She didn't say, "Let me pay you back for all of the money you gave me over the years."

She had that little boy cussing me out and writing

me letters calling me all kinds of names as a deadbeat dad. And I was never his father. And she knew it all along. I understand it from his standpoint. I understand his pain and his anger. He thought I was his daddy and I wasn't there for him. But I can't pretend. He's not my kid. While I feel bad for him, I can't be something to him that I'm not. He has to take that up with his mother.

I had another girlfriend, from Jersey City, whom I was with off and on. I went to grammar school with her and we had known each other for a long time. We got together when I came back from Utah.

I was out of the pros and smoking a lot of weed and dipping and dabbing with cocaine. She came to me and told me she was pregnant. Once again, I was there for the whole thing. I moved in with her. I changed diapers, took care of the baby.

But the DNA test came back and the results were in and . . . I was *not* the father. Again.

The first one took the sting off it. I was prepared this time. Oh, well.

That baby had been named Jeremiah Wright. (What a name, right?) I don't have any contact with these women or the kids anymore. I don't know what it's like to live a lie like that. They have their children going through life thinking one man is their father and the boys even have my name, but that's not who they are. What can you do?

I don't hold grudges. It's less of a headache for me. I

don't have to pay out the money anymore, even though I can't get the money back I paid out. But I don't have to deal with the drama that comes with believing I'm their father. I don't have to subject my wife to that.

My mother knew all along with this one, too. She knew with the first child and she knew with Jeremiah. She took one look at the baby when he was born and said, "Lou, that's not your child."

I said, "You don't know, Ma. Stop saying that. That's my child! Stop saying that."

She was right. I had to go to my mother and say sorry.

My Philly lady and I met at Asbury Park in Jersey at the Greek weekend. Yes, I used to get around. We were engaged to be married. We met shortly after I was drafted at a club one evening. We hit it off. She was my lady while I was playing with the Jazz. She got pregnant the summer I got drafted. I brought her out to Utah to live with me.

My son, Jalil Terrance Wright, was born. I fell in love with that kid. He looked like me and acted like my peoples. I knew he was mine. But I still had to have the DNA test. The results came back and . . . I *am* the father! Jalil is now nearly six feet tall, plays basketball, and is smart and handsome like his dad.

I also have a daughter, Paris. I met her mom in Florida during NBA rookie orientation. She got pregnant that weekend during my three days in Florida. I didn't hear from her much until she told me she was pregnant.

When I saw Paris, I knew she was my daughter. But I had had that feeling before and was wrong. The test showed that my feelings were right. Paris is my daughter. She is a cheerleader/dancer for her high school. She is six feet tall, a beautiful young lady. She has her mother's last name, but I'd like her to change her name to Wright. We have a great relationship and I'm proud of her.

I love being a father. I had a stepdad whom I loved, and I had a mostly great relationship with my own father toward the end of his life. Even though he left my mom when I was twelve, he was there and had an impact on my life. Before he died, we were able to talk, laugh, and cry together. I loved that man.

I love children. But I have to admit that I didn't know how to love women. I used women. I was abusive—not physically—but definitely emotionally. I never learned how to really treat a woman. They were there for my needs, and when I was ready to move on, I would. I didn't think twice.

So while I never ran out on my responsibilities (at least financially) as a dad, I would often leave women without batting an eye.

But that changed when I met Angie.

18) MY GOD

was raised in the church. When I say I was raised in the church, I mean I was literally raised in the church. I had to go to church just about every day. There was prayer meeting, midweek service, Bible study, revival—and on Sunday, it was an all-day affair. I had to go to Sunday school, both services, and if a church choir was visiting, we had to stay for that, too.

I didn't know anything was wrong with it or that people didn't go to church the way I went to church until the kids in my neighborhood started teasing me, calling me Church Boy. But that was my life. So I can say that I always knew God on some level.

I wasn't always His friend, though.

For a long time, I was mad at God. I questioned

whether He loved me. I couldn't understand why He would let certain things happen to me. Why would He let my parents break up? Why didn't He protect me all of those times I was being molested and raped? Why?

But even with my doubts and my anger, I never really walked away from God. He was always in my ear telling me what I should do. I didn't always listen—most of the time I didn't listen. But when I had no place else to turn, I turned back to God.

I was in a crack house and I had just had the surgery on my foot. As I look back on it now, it seems so crazy to get out of surgery and go right back to a crack house. But I didn't know how not to be a crackhead at that point. I didn't know how to do anything else.

Right in that moment at the height of my being lost, God spoke to me. He told me to look at myself. This is not what He made me to be. Throughout my whole experience, I knew God was watching over me, protecting me. God has always been talking to me. But this was the first time in a long time that I was listening.

He was telling me that I wasn't a drug addict. I wasn't a gangbanger. I wasn't a petty thief. I was His child.

Without God, I'd still be smoking crack. I'd still be homeless.

I'm so far removed from that place now. But I don't forget it. The memory keeps my sobriety in front of me.

When I called my cousin to take me away, I found a treatment center. I had been down that road before. This time I was traveling with God and I was serious and determined not to go back to that life or the streets no matter how bad things got. I was going to face it.

When I was in recovery in the past, I knew in the back of my mind it was temporary. I went through the motions the whole time knowing I would be back to smoking weed, back to smoking crack, back to running away. This time, I knew this was it, and it was scarier than anything else I've been through. The withdrawal was crazy. It wasn't a physical withdrawal from drugs. That part was actually easy. It was the emotional withdrawal that I deal with even today. The craving. The wanting to do it and knowing that I can't. I won't.

I'm in recovery every day. Every single day. I make sure that I spend time with other recovering addicts because I can't get too comfortable thinking that I can beat this on my own. Life is a recovery process.

I used to get clean for a few months, then go right back to smoking. I was even clean for more than a year one time, and then something happened (I don't even remember what it was), and I went right back to crack as if I'd never stopped.

I called it taking a break. But I would always go back to smoking. I checked into a hospital for six months because I was tired. But as soon as I got out, I was right back on the streets, looking to get high. I wasn't committed to recovery.

It seemed as if I did that forever—getting clean, going back, getting clean, going back. I never took my clean time seriously. I was labeled a menace to society because of my mental health. So I just went with it.

But this last time, this final time, God was whispering and I was listening. For the first time in a long time I was clear about what I needed to do. Here I was missing two toes, blowing my chances to ever go back to basketball. I was out millions of dollars and I had these kids. I had children out there that I wasn't taking care of. I wanted to know my kids. And I wanted them to know me—not this crackhead, homeless dude.

I was sick. I was sick and tired of being homeless. Sick and tired of being high.

You have to get to a point of being sick and tired. Something has to come out of it, unless you're an idiot.

This wasn't a different recovery program. All of those are pretty much the same. This was a different me. It was my different approach to recovery that produced the results.

Narcotics Anonymous. I had been to it before. I knew the routine. But this time, I was taking it seriously. When I would say, "I'm Luther Wright and I'm an addict," I meant it this time. I couldn't really say those words before and mean it. I had to say it and know that it was me I was talking about.

Before in recovery, I would compare my addiction to those of others and say, "I may smoke coke, but I ain't sniffing it," or, "I drink 151, I don't drink vodka or

Hennessy," or, "At least I'm not a heroin addict. That's really bad!"

I was comparing notes with other addicts and giving myself a pass to get high because I wasn't a dope fiend and nodding on the corner. I functioned pretty well. I was not as bad as *that* guy.

April 6, 2006, midnight, I was one year clean. I celebrated by going to my meeting and going to get something to eat. That day, I knew I would probably never take drugs again. It took one whole year for me to feel confident that I could actually do this.

After I went out to eat, I decided to take up a friend of mine on an offer he had been making forever to go to his church. I had been resisting going to church with Stanley for a couple of reasons. One reason was because when you're a kid, you *have* to do something because they say so. Well, when I was old enough to say no, I stopped going. When I was old enough to make my own decisions, I decided not to go back.

Another reason was that I thought I knew what "church" was all about, and I didn't want any part of it. I had seen too many church folks be hypocrites, praising the Lord and catching the Holy Ghost on Sundays and sinning Monday through Saturday. I had seen too many pastors who would say one thing in the pulpit and do something different at home. Or worse.

But Stanley was persistent. He kept telling me how wonderful his church was, so I decided to see for myself. This time when he asked, I finally said yes. I felt as if maybe I needed to be in church. I also knew that I shouldn't put my faith in man because man will disappoint you every time. I needed to put my faith in God. I needed to not worry about what people are doing or not doing.

That first experience at Morning Star confirmed that I had been missing the point all of these years. That first service was so different from what I expected. The people weren't what I expected. It wasn't the way it was when I was a kid. These people seemed serious about serving the Lord. And there was so much love there.

When the congregation recited their affirmation— "I am filled with and led by God's Holy Spirit. I am learning and living in God's Holy Word. I believe in and model Jesus Christ, our Lord. I'm here to make a positive difference and I have a passion for mission"—I could tell that they meant it. I could feel it throughout this average-size church on Chandler Avenue in Linden, New Jersey. It was nothing special from the outside. But on the inside I could feel God.

This was different from what I had seen growing up with people getting the Holy Ghost and carrying on— but then having rent parties and cussing and drinking and smoking. People were sober at Morning Star. People knew what they were coming to the Lord for. And the pastor was about teaching the Word. Not just preaching and carrying on from the pulpit. People were in their Bibles with highlighters and notebooks. We studied the

Bible at Morning Star. It was about the Word, not about a whole lot of feelings and emotions.

I felt at home from day one. You know how you go somewhere and people treat you like you're special, like you matter? I felt that way at Morning Star, and it had nothing to do with my being an NBA basketball player. Most of the people didn't even know that I'd played basketball—which was weird, as tall as I was. But they didn't care. I was Brother Luther. Not Lou Bee or Big Lou. I was their brother in Christ and they loved me not because I could dunk a basketball or block a shot.

That first time there, I remember thinking afterward, *I needed that!* I was hungry for more. I didn't want it to be over. So I kept coming back. A week later, I actually joined.

I didn't just join and sit in the pew and be fed every week. I got involved. I joined the choir. I got involved with the homeless ministry. I got involved with the youth ministry. I was in it 100 percent.

I went from showing up just on Sundays to being at church every day. How ironic. The very thing I used to hate, I now loved. I would wake up looking forward to going to church because I was involved. That became my home.

I was living in a halfway house after leaving recovery. No way was I going back to my mother's house. I knew my recovery wouldn't last if I went back to that. Then I finally got my own place—a small apartment in Elizabeth in a bad neighborhood, not far from my church in Linden. But I didn't spend much time there. I was always at Morning Star.

Once a week, our men's ministry would patrol the neighborhood around the church. There would be twelve to sixteen of us and it was good because the kids on the corner showed respect. We would talk to them and mentor them, and crime in the area went down dramatically. I liked making a difference. We'd run into some homeless people and some drug addicts out there. I used to be one of those people. Now I was out there helping. I could relate and I could speak to them unlike anyone else.

This felt better than any crowd cheering my name on the basketball court or waving it like they just didn't care on the dance floor. This felt good in a deep place inside me. The cheers and the accolades fade. But touching someone's life and living for Christ, that feeling never fades.

To be able to express myself through basketball, through music, and now through this book is a blessing. Just sitting in my neighborhood and have kids coming up to me and talk and being able to share with them my experiences is great. I help them not to make the same mistakes I made.

I started coaching basketball in 2009. I got to appreciate all of the coaches that I gave a hard time to. It's so much easier to see yourself when you're on the other side. Being the type of player and person I was made it easier for me to reach some of the players. I could give them real talk that they could understand.

I realize how much I have to offer. I can give a kid from a neighborhood like the one I came from a chance to get an education. I tell them to appreciate that chance because I didn't. And they're listening.

I know all of that is God.

After I completely devoted my life to God, He decided to rain down a few blessings on me. One of them, which I didn't expect at all, was named Angie.

19) NO MORE GAME

met Angie at Morning Star Community Christian
Center (the church I still attend) in Linden, New
Jersey. I had seen her around. We were in the choir
together. I was also in the band. When I joined the
choir, she came up to me and said, "Hi, brother. How're
you doing? Welcome to the choir."

I thought she was nice, but I could never see myself
with her. I couldn't see myself with anyone. I mean,
think about where I was coming from. I had been on
the streets for so long. I looked a mess—my teeth
were missing, and I had put on a lot of weight. I didn't
have a job or any money. I didn't even have a car to get
around in. A girlfriend? That wasn't a possibility, or so
I thought.

But I remember the night when I became open to the idea.

Every Friday, about sixteen men from our church would meet at the church, then we would walk through the community, passing out flyers for our church events and just kind of patrolling, picking up trash, talking to the kids who might be hanging out on the corners. We were about showing a strong male presence in the community.

This particular night, Men's Fellowship was canceled, but nobody told me. (I was hard to reach because I didn't have a phone.) I showed up. I caught a ride from someone and was stuck because I didn't have a ride back home. So I decided to hang out with the youth group.

I noticed Angie immediately. She was running around with the kids, playing kickball as if she were one of them. That smile really caught my attention. I couldn't take my eyes off her.

Angie tells the story better than I do, but I also remember her outfit. It was red and right. It was fitting her. I was like "Wow!"

I was impressed because she was pretty and athletic. She played every position in the game. She was all over the field.

When the game was over, I went over and said something to her. I can't remember what I said, but I know I struck up a conversation. I think I told her that I was stranded because she offered me a ride home. That, too, was impressive. She had this tiny black Hyundai

Tiburon, which by normal standards was small, but it was supersmall considering that I had to squeeze my seven-foot-two-inch, nearly four-hundred-pound frame into it.

She didn't even flinch when I squeezed myself into the subcompact.

I was living in this run-down place in Elizabeth and was too embarrassed for her to see how I was living. The week before, one of the brothers who was hanging out front with me got robbed. They didn't mess with me, but I definitely didn't want to put Angie in any danger. Just thinking about her dropping me off there made me know that I had to move. You can get comfortable in a place, and I knew what that felt like. That attitude was taking me back to my days of being homeless, and I wasn't going back. This was what I could afford, but I knew I could do better. So my first order of business was to move.

I told Angie to drop me off several blocks from where I was staying. After she pulled over to let me out, I ended up sitting in that tiny car and talking for more than two hours with my knees in my chest. I told her everything that night. Everything.

"I gotta tell you this," I said. "I come from a dysfunctional family. I got robbed. I had a boatload of money. I used to be in the NBA. This is where I'm at. I used to like to get high. I used to be homeless. I'm trying to get it together."

I told it all. She didn't flinch.

I even told her about my kids and the whole craziness with the baby-mama drama. I also told her that the next woman I went out with, I was going to marry. She didn't flinch at that either.

I had dated some duds. I was a dud when I was with them. But this woman was something special. I don't know what it was about her, but being around her was like taking some sort of truth serum and I didn't want to run any game on her.

I was never one to talk a lot, but this night with this woman, I was telling it all.

I was so nervous, too, just being around her. I didn't think I would stand a chance with Angie because of the way she carries herself. Here I was just a year away from homelessness. I'm missing my front teeth. I'm missing two toes. I'm not raking in the dough anymore. But she didn't push me away. She listened. She looked at me as if she was seeing me beyond all of that stuff I was telling her about who I was.

She just sat there, taking it all in. I kept it real with her—something I had never done with any other woman.

When we were done talking, I got out and walked the few blocks to where I was staying. I knew I needed to make some real changes—and moving was the first change I needed to make.

Angie gave me her phone number, and when I tried to call her, she seemed to never be around. She had gone out of town and I didn't hear from her. I didn't know she'd gone out of town; I just thought that maybe I scared her away, telling her everything during that first night.

But something inside told me that it would be okay. We had instant chemistry.

I'd played out many women. But Angie was different. She was just so nice. She's a sweetheart. I never met a woman like her before, ever. In all of my years on this planet, Angie is the only woman I've ever met that I just had to love. The only other woman that I had to love and didn't have a choice is my mother.

Angie made me see the world differently. She is such a lady that she helped me see the world from a woman's perspective. And she wasn't a gold digger. She liked me for me. Not for my basketball skills or because of my popularity. Not for my money and fame. But for me.

If I had an issue or a strong opinion about something, I would talk it over with Angie, and she would make me see it from the other side. That was amazing in itself. I never had anybody in my life whom I respected enough to listen to. Maybe it was because Angie was older than me. She had been through a lot herself, so I later found out. She had been in the army, lived all over the country, then come back to Jersey City. She had been married before. She was definitely different.

I was just amazed by her. I tell her that all the time.

"You knock me off my feet!" I tell her.

It was her spirit.

I felt something about Angie. I had a long talk with myself. I said, "Don't hold nothing back. The good, the bad, the ugly." The next girl who was wife material I was going to tell it all. I was ready to find a mate. I had got out of the program. I had my own place. I was handling my business. Working, volunteering. But I didn't have a friend. I didn't have a partner. I didn't feel fulfilled. I wanted to share my experiences and be with somebody. I met Angie.

We took it slow.

I started dating her in August 2006.

We started talking on the phone. It got to be that we would talk every single night for hours. Our first real date out was to see *Idlewild*, that movie starring Outkast. We went to Wendy's for a bite to eat afterward. After that date, it was a wrap. She was falling for me. I'd already fallen.

On Sundays, I would just be beaming watching her sing in the choir. She has some voice. We would do a lot of church functions together. It helped that she was active in the church and we got to spend more and more time together.

I proposed to her in January. I'd known in November that she was going to be my wife.

In November, my sister passed away. I was a year and a few months clean. My sister's passing almost sent me backward. That would have been a perfect opportunity to backslide, a perfect excuse.

When that ball dropped in my lap, Angie didn't say, "Let's have a drink." She said, "Call pastor."

Angie gave me food for thought. If I had taken it to my homeboys, I would probably have relapsed. Angie had the right answers. She was there from the time my sister passed until we buried her. Angie had my back.

I ended up moving in with Angie because I didn't want to be alone during that time. As I was looking for the next place to live, it just seemed natural to live with her. We were spending just about every waking moment together anyway.

But being that we were both in the church, it just didn't look right. Angie definitely didn't like being my "girlfriend." But from the moment I moved in, I had planned on making her my wife.

I knew I had to have my stuff together first. This time, I wanted to make sure I had a plan. We were living together for convenience and because I didn't feel safe staying anyplace else. But marriage was for keeps.

I talked to my pastor about it and told him that I was going to ask Angie to be my wife. I wanted it to be memorable and special. He was in on it from the beginning.

We were having Bible study on Thursday. I went to Zales that afternoon and got the ring. I had picked it out weeks before, but had to wait until I had the money. My spiritual father, Clinton Hardy, went with me to get it.

I knew Angie was going to say yes. I kept saying to her, "I'm going to marry you," and, "Are you going to marry me?" This was a constant. She would just smile.

Before Bible study, I met with the pastor and mapped

out how it was going to go down. At the beginning of Bible study, he said, "Somebody in here has an important question to ask. I feel it. I just know somebody is going to ask a question."

Nobody asked a question. Pastor went on and taught his lesson. When he was done, I raised my hand.

"Brother Luther, you got a question you want to ask?" he said.

"Yes, this question is for Sister Angela Felton," I said, walking around to where she was sitting.

I got down on one knee in front of her, pulled her ring out of my pocket, and said, "Will you marry me?"

The whole church broke out into oohs and aahs. Old ladies were crying. Angie was crying.

I knew God sent her to me. I knew I couldn't mess this one up. She was the one. I'm trying to explain this in words. But being with Angie is so much deeper than any words can express. She is the most special person I have ever known. She makes me want to be better.

We got married in 2007. It was a simple wedding performed by our pastor at Costa del Sol in Union, New Jersey. We didn't spend a whole lot of money. We knew we didn't need a big wedding to seal our bond. It was already sealed.

Since we've been married, we haven't had any real arguments, no real conflicts. If we have any issues, I say to her, "Babe, we got to talk." And she will say, "What's up?" And we handle it. We squash it before it turns into anything. We communicate. We talk. We don't let things go. That honesty that I started off the relationship with is the honesty that we live by.

I have no desire to fight with her about anything, and she's so easygoing that no matter what I do or say, she just rolls with it. I get to see what unconditional love means through her.

I can't stay mad at her. I tried once. One morning, we were running late and she had to drop me off at the Holland Tunnel for an appointment. She wasn't driving the way I wanted, and dropping me off was out of her way. It would make her a half hour late for work. Instead of understanding, when a turn came that I thought she should take to get us there quicker, I yelled, "Yo, what're you doing!"

She didn't say a word. She calmly turned around and went the way I wanted her to turn. I felt like a jerk. She dropped me off and said good-bye as if it were all good, which made it worse. Five minutes later, I texted her that I was sorry. I had to apologize. My insides were eating me up.

Old Luther never apologized and didn't care. I never knew how to express being wrong without giving up something. But with Angie, I've learned that it's okay to be wrong. It's okay to say sorry. It doesn't take away from my manhood. And I feel better. If you can't let bygones be bygones or say "My bad" or "I'm sorry" when it's appropriate, then you really aren't much of a man.

I don't have to ask Angie if she loves me. I know she does. She does things for me that no one has ever before done for me. She oils my feet—and pays special attention to the area where my toes used to be. She washes my clothes. She cooks for me. She be hooking it up. She can whip something together in forty-five minutes that's just banging. It's not the things she does, though. It's just how she is. I'm in love.

More than that, she knows how to deal with me. You know how they say there are two sides to every story. She makes me see both sides. She opens my third eye.

With Angie, I knew I didn't have to hide who I am or who I was. I didn't have to try to fit into her world. I just did. I knew that I could have peace with her. I could be myself, and I could grow with her. I didn't want to get with a person whom I had to teach something. I've spent these years learning.

The biggest thing I learned being with Angie was how to love.

I never knew a marriage could be like this. I guess I never took the time to get to know a woman or be into a woman like this. But it's amazing.

We're doing it the way God would want us to—in the church. If we do have a problem, we take it to God.

With Angie I had the chance to rewind my life. It was a fresh start and I was going to do some things (a whole bunch of things) differently. I may have blown many opportunities and millions of dollars, but I was smart enough this time around to know that I didn't want to blow it with Angie. I was finally going to get something right!

AFTERWORD

by Terry Cummings

I met Luther at the 2010 NBA All-Star Game in Dallas. We were part of a group of former NBA players who would perform (singing, playing instruments, etc.) in a sort of a band during All-Star Weekend. Luther and I spent a lot of time together in the week leading up to the games. If we weren't rehearsing for our performance, we were sitting down somewhere breaking bread.

We instantly hit it off because we had a lot in common—mainly the Lord. But it was when Luther started to share his story that we really bonded.

I remember him from the league. While our career paths never crossed directly, I did hear about what had happened to him. But as Luther was telling me the details, I was reminded that his story is not so unusual in the world of sports. Sure, the details may be horrific, but what led Luther to that point, unfortunately, is there for so many young athletes today.

The athlete in society is treated like the prince of the kingdom. We see it from itty-bitty ball, through grade school, high school, and to the pros. They are praised, coddled, and put on pedestals. They get to feel the appreciation and the roar of the crowd, and it becomes addictive.

But what happens when the cheering stops? What happens when that athlete is no longer the star? What happens when he has to go back to being just a regular person? Luther Wright is an extreme example of what happens. But it happens every day in some form.

From the grade-school superstar that never quite makes it in high school, to the high-school superstar who doesn't make it to college, to the college standout who goes bust in the NBA, it's the same story.

I liken it to a sort of postwar syndrome, where the soldiers come home from war and can't adjust to regular society. Their minds are so twisted by the things they saw on the battlefield—the rush of going on a mission—that they can't go back to being normal.

For the athlete, when their playing days are over and they have to go back into society as a "normal" person, many can't cope. If a kid was a college star and makes it to the NBA, he expects to be a star there, too. He was "the man" on his college team, yet in the NBA he is faced with the reality that just about everybody there is as good or better than he is. That's tough for some, for most. Many rookies can't make the adjustment. They don't know what it's like to be "regular" or "normal" or "just like everybody else."

I believe this is what happened to Luther. He was a star in college and came to a team of veterans where he would have to be a role player. He went from superstar to bench player and, coupled with all of the other pressures performing in the NBA brings, it was too much. I saw it a lot. Many players didn't lose it in quite the same way, but I certainly understand how it could happen.

I was blessed. When I came into the league, I had a great support system. When I was traded to the Milwaukee Bucks after my rookie season, it couldn't have been a better situation for me. As a young player, the Bucks were a team of veterans, but their mentality was family comes first. They taught me how to adjust to the NBA; they took me under their wing, and I would spend a lot of time with their families. They even taught me how to shop and what to wear. I loved it when we played the Philadelphia 76ers because the whole team would go to Boyds, a three-level clothing store, and we would practically shut the place down.

They taught me how to handle playing in the NBA, and I carried that attitude to every team I played on. I felt it was my responsibility to help shepherd these young players along and help them make it. It got to the point that, later in my career, after I had gotten injured and couldn't play at an All-Star level every night, teams would still trade for me because of what I would bring in terms of helping their younger players. They saw value in how I was able to relate to them and bring stability to a team, teach them how to be men in the league, but more importantly how to be men off the court.

When I was brought on to play for the Seattle Supersonics, they had two stars in Vin Baker and Glenn Robinson, with whom I bumped heads immediately. We even went toe-to-toe at one point. But when the dust cleared, they had an understanding of what was acceptable behavior for a professional player, and the team didn't have any more problems out of them.

We *are* our brothers' keepers.

A lot of these players were raised without a father. For them, I wasn't just a big brother but a father figure. And I accepted this role because I believed it made my team better to watch out and watch over the other players. But it was also my duty as a man to not let any of my brothers fall.

For Luther, perhaps there weren't any players or coaches around who he respected enough to listen to. I don't know, because I didn't know Luther then. But I know him today.

There are a lot of Luthers out there. They are struggling with an identity crisis, trying to find their way. His story will help them. It can also benefit those who are straight. All of us think we all have it together. In life, you're really only one hand away from someone pulling you or pushing you from failure or success. His story is a reminder of that. It is also a reminder of where your source of dependence should be.

For a lot of players, they've had people in their lives that were only there to take. They've had mentors who were only mentoring them for what they could get from that player. They've had coaches who only cared about winning championships, but didn't care about the player himself.

I know it's easy for a player to grow cynical and not trust anyone—not even his own family sometimes. This dictates how that kid perceives the world. It's kill or be killed. Eat or be eaten. And this attitude can make for a very twisted view of the world and have you feeling you are in this battle alone.

Luther had that view for a while. But God gave him grace and Luther took advantage of it. A lot of cats don't get the second chance Luther got. Some of them are dead. But he was given this chance for a reason. For his testimony.

To hear it, right down to losing part of his foot, and to be with him and experience his personality, his happy-go-lucky way, is truly a blessing.

I can't say that I know what it feels like to walk in Luther's shoes or experience his journey; but knowing about affliction, persecution and suffering, I know that it leaves marks on your life. I know that those experiences shape us—oftentimes in a very negative way.

Luther could easily look back on his life and at what he lost, and be bitter. But he's just the opposite. When you sit down and talk to Lu, you just fall in love with him. He has this big kid inside and that big kid is alive and having fun. That big kid is living life. He doesn't wear the scars from his past. He doesn't carry the baggage of bad decisions and busted dreams. He is living his life with the fruit of the spirit.

If you spend just a little time with Luther, what you walk away with is the knowledge that God is awesome. That He can take a life, a story like Luther's, and turn it around to be a blessing for others.

Terry Cummings played in the National Basketball League for eighteen seasons. Drafted by the San Diego Clippers, he was the 1982–1983 Rookie of the Year. He would play for six more teams, including the Philadelphia 76ers and the New York Knicks. He was also a two-time All-Star for the Milwaukee Bucks. Cummings, who is heavily involved in music, is also an ordained minister who pastors a church in Atlanta, Georgia. He has three sons.